IS ANYBODY THERE?
DOES ANYBODY CARE?

ROBERT LAROCHELLE

ENERGION PUBLICATIONS
Gonzalez, Florida
2023

ISBN: 978-1-63199-869-0
eISBN: 978-1-63199-870-6

Energion Publications
P. O. Box 841
Gonzalez, FL 32560

energion.com
pubs@energion.com

This book is dedicated to my wife
Patricia Coppinger LaRochelle.
It is with profound gratitude
for our 42 years of married life together!

INTRODUCTION

Is Anybody There? Does Anybody Care?

This is a book that I never expected to write as I had thought that my days of writing books were well in my past. As a matter of fact, I was quite pleased that as recently as 2022 I was able to have a brand new book published entitled *I Love the Church, I Hate the Church: Paradox or Contradiction*[1] as well as an updated edition of my book *Crossing the Street.*[2] Both of these books were born out of my own personal experiences with organized religion and I wrote them as resources for people to explore in considerable depth as they examined the place of religion in their own lives. When I finished writing them, I was content that I had covered a lot of topics that I considered to be quite important. I also hoped that perhaps folks would read these books and have some lively conversations with others about what was contained therein.

As I write this, I have just reached the milestone of being seventy years old! Consequently, it made a lot of sense to conclude that after forty three years of working in the field of education, coupled with an active life as an ordained clergyperson in both Roman Catholic and Protestant congregations since 1989, that this would not be the time to get involved in writing another book to add to

---

1   Published by Wipf and Stock (2021).
2   Published by Energion Publications (new second edition, 2021).

my previous ones. [3] After all, I have already retired from my work as a teacher and counselor and am no longer serving as a pastor of any church. [4] In fact, I have felt that as I have entered this latest phase of my life, it was perfectly acceptable to face the reality that my days of turning out new books were well in the past. I was very much at peace with that fact!

However, I have come to discover that while I have formally retired from serving churches as their pastor, I have clearly NOT retired from thinking about the church, the subject of so many of my previous writings.

Organized Christian faith remains very important to me and plays a significant role in my life. Such has been the case from my childhood days when I was an active Catholic altar boy and has continued right through my evolving years as an adult as much of my study and my professional involvement has centered on activities connected with this rather unique institution that goes by the name of *church*. [5] It was also an important part of my educational background which included considerable study in the area of religion. [6] Consequently, I came to discover that despite my retired status, I still had a lot of things about organized religion and "the church" that I wanted to say!

It is important to note that I have written this book at a time in my life when I have been doing a good amount of traveling around and preaching in a rather large number of churches and specifically in those communities of faith in two different denominations.

---

3   Overall, I had written eight books, including *Part Time Pastor, Full Time Church*, which was my first. *It was published by Pilgrim Press in 2011.*

4   I have served churches in Connecticut which have been part of both the United Church of Christ and the Evangelical Lutheran Church in America.

5   When I use the word church, I am referring to a community of people. I am NOT referring to a building. This usage is very intentional as it reflects my theology of church, i.e. ecclesiology.

6   My academic background includes an undergraduate degree in Religious Studies, a Master's in Religious Education and a Doctor of Ministry degree in preaching. In addition, I also hold a Master's degree in Counseling.

These two are the Evangelical Lutheran Church in America and the United Church of Christ[7]. Those of you who have read my previous books know that raised a Roman Catholic, I served for several years as an ordained Permanent Deacon[8] and when I left the Catholic Church in 1998, I eventually proceeded to serve churches in both the ELCA and UCC. In 2002, I was ordained as a minister in the United Church of Christ [9]and I have also been able to serve as a pastor in Lutheran congregations because of the Formula of Agreement among several mainline Protestant churches.[10]

It has been my experience in traveling to congregations in different denominations, coupled with that of reflecting on my days of growing up Roman Catholic and serving in ordained ministry within that church tradition, that led me to the conviction that this would be a worthwhile book to write at this point in both my own life and that of the institutional church.

Let me tell you why:

In reading this book, you will see what you most likely know, at least on some visceral level. *What you will both notice and probably find reinforced in my writing is that organized Christianity as expressed through the institution known as church is experiencing significant decline in the United States, as well as in many other parts of the world.* This is a widely acknowledged fact, one which I explore in considerable detail within the chapters of this book. In reflecting both on the available data and upon my own experience in traveling to a rather large number of church congregations quite regularly

---

7   These denominations are deeply rooted in the history of religion in the United States.

8   Within Roman Catholicism, the three recognized ordained ministries are those of bishop, priest and deacon. I was ordained to the order of deacon in June 1989 at the Cathedral of St. Joseph in Hartford, Connecticut. Within Catholicism, a deacon can baptize, officiate at weddings and funerals, and preach, in addition to several other responsibilities.

9   I was ordained at First Congregational Church of Vernon, Connecticut, United Church of Christ (UCC).

10 The Formula of Agreement provides a process whereby clergy in certain denominations may also lead worship and possibly serve as pastors in other denominations which are part of this agreement.

as a visitor who is there to lead worship and to preach, I have observed that the decline in church attendance has been obvious. It is something I have witnessed with my own eyes as I have looked out into the congregations with whom I have been worshiping and have taken notice of all the empty pews right in front of me. Oftentimes, in these moments, I cannot help but think back to the days when it was quite typical for pews in churches to be quite full. In addition, over these last few years, in traveling to these many churches, I have discovered that in a great number of them, *very few children or adolescents are to be found either in the pews or in their nurseries.* To the contrary, I have found many congregations to be mostly composed of people of my own age or older!

In conversations with pastors, I have become quite aware of the fact that there has been a significant decline in the number of young people for whom participation in church activities is a part of their lives. As is the case with many of their parents, their weekends are spent in a variety of other activities with attendance at worship not being among them.

In addition, at the same time, I have also noticed some other things that have been happening in churches around me in Connecticut and nearby Massachusetts, most specifically in those churches I have served within the Evangelical Lutheran Church in America. In fact, an ELCA[11] congregation at which I was pastor for three years closed its doors only five years after I left, another congregation at which I had recently officiated at a funeral shut down just a few weeks before I started writing this book and a nearby church not far from where I live closed not that long ago. These examples only scratch the surface as church closures have become quite typical in the life of some denominations. To be quite honest, the realities connected with these closures have left me deeply concerned.

Now, as you will see throughout this book, there are several different ways in which one could look at these realities of church attendance decline and increasing closures:

---

11 Evangelical Lutheran Church in America.

1. You could say that when a congregation is dwindling in attendance, it makes sense to admit that it may be time for the congregation to close and to celebrate what it has done in the time it was around. I have found this to be an integral part of planning for the eventual affirmation of a church's closure.[12]

2. OR INSTEAD, you could say that because of the closing, the opportunities for people to explore the spiritual strengths of that denomination have been thwarted. In fact, I would contend that if "mainline" [13] Christian churches close down at the same time as more conservative evangelical churches in their communities remain open, the overall loss is extremely significant and not to be taken lightly.

3. In reading this book, you will find that I have some real concerns about the explosion in the number of *"conservative"* and *"independent"* Christian churches[14]. I express these concerns within the context of my deeply seated feelings and thoughts about closures in mainline churches.

A SUBJECT FOR SERIOUS CONCERN ...

Throughout the time that I have served as a pastor in mainline Protestant churches, these concerns of mine have increased quite considerably. *I worry about the local mainline congregations the wider church is losing and am greatly troubled as well about what is happening in many of the other expressions of Christianity that remain in place and may also be showing some growth.* [15]

---

12 This can be a very intense period in a church's life, for sure!!

13 Mainline churches include the ELCA, UCC, Episcopal Church, Disciples of Christ, Presbyterian Church USA, as well as several others.

14 These are churches that are connected with one another in their approach to the Bible and theology but are not part of the mainline denominations. These churches approach the Bible from a position quite different from that of mainline churches.

15 I am concerned about the high level of fundamentalism in those churches as well as their inadequate study of Biblical texts.

It is that inner passion for the importance of what we call mainline Christianity[16] which I have felt which is expressed in the sermons that I preach as well as the words I have spoken at various meetings in churches I served prior to my retirement. This was the impetus that has led me to the conviction that it was important to write yet another book, the one you are beginning to read at this moment.

In a very real sense, this book builds upon much of my previous writing, as well as the speaking I have done within churches I have served as both a settled[17] and guest pastor. However, I have written it with an urgency that while definitely present in some of my other books, has now moved to a different and more intense level as I have entered the world of being a senior citizen with most of my professional work well situated in my past. Consequently, I write this book to engage people in serious conversations about the future of the church and, where necessary, to encourage people to slow down and think through what it means to close a congregation and to consider carefully the pros and cons attached to keeping a church open.

To be honest, you will see in this book something of a clarion call to explore what can be done to keep mainline churches vibrant and alive! One of my goals in writing this book is quite simply that it will be a helpful and practical resource for conversations within churches while they are still around!

- As you will most likely notice from reading this book, I come out of the experience of working in middle schools and high schools for a period of forty- three years. This experience has been very helpful to me in my work as a pastor. [18] During that

---

16 This includes denominations I have mentioned previously, two examples of which are the UCC and the ELCA.

17 This would be a pastor who has a contractual obligation to serve in this ministry within the congregation. Most recently, a great number of churches have also been employing interim pastors.

18 I taught religion for several years in Catholic schools and served as a School Counselor for thirty years. Most of my time as a Counselor was in

time, I have sat through a lot of presentations that have been driven by various current trends in education. Some of those trends have been valuable, for sure, but the reality is that many have been long gone and forgotten.

- I remember with something less than fondness a time when I and seven or eight other colleagues from a middle school in which I worked attended a workshop for an entire week which took place forty miles away and focused on a brand new program for teenagers that the workshop leaders were convinced was important and should be implemented in schools throughout both our state and our nation.

- Now, the cost of sending teachers, counselors and administrators to these workshops involved thousands of dollars. After the initial excitement attached to it had faded, the program completely fell by the wayside and was never really implemented as planned. It was never to be presented again as part of the school's curriculum. This situation exemplified some of the problems that can emerge within school settings. What I am describing here occurred when I first made the move from working at a private parochial school and ended up being hired as a Counselor in a public school.[19]

- This was a five-day program which took place a good distance away from where I lived. Between the actual cost of the program and the mileage reimbursement for staff members who attended, the cost accrued by the district was quite considerable! As I have noted, I wish I could say that these were the only examples of what I experienced in my career in education. Sadly, they are not!

In addition, even prior to this, at the time when I began a new job within a public school where I lived, the school district spent considerable money sending me along with other staff members

---

public schools in Connecticut.

19 Timothy Edward Middle School, South Windsor, Connecticut.

to a weeklong program which was a training session for those of us implementing the QUEST [20] program in our middle school.

Well intentioned as it was, as it turned out, the counselors involved in implementing the program for sixth graders, such as I, had to teach that QUEST centered class during the time set aside in that school day wherein the counselor and the team of teachers assigned to students were expected to meet with parents who wished to have PPTs and other related meetings.[21]

I discovered quite quickly that even though I was fairly young at the time, I did not possess the gift of bilocation! While parents were meeting with teachers, they were also wondering where the counselor of their child happened to be. In addition, the teachers got frustrated that I was not present as well. Of course, I couldn't be unless I wanted to risk the possibility of leaving 25 sixth graders alone for forty-five minutes in a classroom which was unsupervised!

All kidding aside, the result of this was both that of making it extremely difficult to establish necessary conversations and relationships between teachers and the counselor and also to make parent/counselor interaction difficult as well. Unintentionally, I was placed in a situation in which the teachers on the team[22] had to explain to parents why their child's Counselor was unable to attend this important meeting. After many years working in parochial schools, which, as is the case with most institutions, had their own set of issues, here was my welcome to the life of public school education! For better or worse, that has become for me the classic example of mismanagement in education. It was not to be the last, for sure!

So... What's my point? What has this apparent diversion got to do with CHURCH?

---

20 QUEST was a program which focused on middle school students and included issues related to self esteem and making positive choices. In our district, it was taught by local police officers who served in our middle school.

21 This strikes me as a classic case of not completely thinking through all the logistics that must be involved.

22 Middle schools are often built on the "team model".

- *In my view, mainline Christian churches need to be exceptionally cautious about church closures.* The very possibility that a church MIGHT have to close has to be examined carefully, contextually and cautiously.[23] This would be as carefully and rigorously as what administrators need to do in suggesting and supporting programs for their teachers and counselors in their public or private school setting. The bottom line is that decisions that flow from legitimate interests and concerns must be thought through completely and with a focus on accessing all of the necessary data and feedback which would lead to a wise decision!

- Churches need to consider the impact of closing "houses of worship" in particular neighborhoods and communities. In doing so, they must also take into account the void with which not only the church members but also others who live in that community would be left. Just as those responsible for scheduling classes during my middle school experience had to see the big picture, so too do those charged with the task of providing leadership within this institution that goes by the name of church.

- One must NEVER underestimate the importance of seeing the larger, wider picture, regardless of the context in which one is working.[24]

In addition, when a mainline church closes and is replaced by a more conservative congregation, that congregation not only replaces the church physically but also takes away from people an approach to Christianity that the mainline church provided. This is an issue that has become increasingly important to me in these last few years. I have seen churches that never even got started

---

23　This cannot be done lightly or at the peak of excitement about a new idea or program, a situation I have witnessed often in my many years of working in the field of education.

24　Over time, I have come to realize how much I learned about church leadership through my experiences in public education such as the one I have described above!

until the 1950's now finding themselves closing and fading away within the communities that they have served. [25] Many of these buildings, in turn, have been replaced by conservative evangelical and fundamentalist churches. This is a matter of deep concern to me as you will see in going through this book!

In this book I will explore these issues in detail. I will do my best to offer opinions based upon both my own learning and my experience as a pastor in different and varied church traditions. In doing so, I have structured this book as follows:

- In Chapter 1, I look at the realities of changes within the institutional church. I have entitled this chapter *"How the Times Have Changed."*
- Chapter 2 details my concerns about what I call the *"clear and present danger"* taking place in churches currently. This explores some of the problems inherent in the loss of many mainline churches and the comparative growth of independent and "evangelical" churches.
- In Chapter 3 I make a case for the importance of Youth Ministry in mainline churches.
- I have entitled Chapter 4 as *"Farewell to Nostalgia"* and in it I examine the ways in which churches are often caught in a nostalgia trap, making peace with having always done things in a certain way. Bob Dylan's song *The Times Are a Changin*[26] is certainly a relevant resource here.
- Chapter 5 is entitled *"Making Peace with Closure: Good or Bad?"* It addresses the dynamics involved in this difficult process that, unfortunately, a large number of churches have gone through over these past few years.
- Chapter 6 offers a reality check regarding church, adolescents and young adults.
- Chapter 7 explores the battle over Pope Francis within Catholicism. In exploring that, I will also explain its relevance

---

25 In my geographical area, I have seen this in several mainline churches.
26 Dylan.

to the overall theme of this book as well as some engagement in speculation about the church's future.

- Chapter 8 centers on the significance of *"Reclaiming Spirituality"*.
- In Chapter 9, I focus on "Rethinking Religious Education." In it, I stress the significance of BOTH adult and *adolescent religious studies with*in the congregation with a recognition as well of the importance of religious education for children.
- Chapter 10 lays out some specific practical suggestions for church life and this final chapter is based on the book's title and brings us back to the question that drove me to write this book : *Is Anybody There? Does Anybody Care?*

What you will discover in these next few pages is that I have a passion for both the presence of AS WELL AS the renewal of the local mainline church. This renewal can best be forged by thinking through difficult questions and engaging in serious conversations about them. My underlying assumption is that this process is one driven by a deep sense of CARING. It is a caring for the place of Christianity and its churches within our communities and in our lives.

It is my hope that this book will be both a resource for your own reflection and provide opportunity for worthwhile conversations among people who care about the church and are committed to its ongoing relevance!

•

1

HOW THE TIMES HAVE CHANGED ...

"In my little town, I grew up believing that God keeps His eyes on us all"- Paul Simon [27]

I grew up in the small Northeastern Connecticut town of Putnam, Connecticut. Except for a brief period in the late 1970's when I spent some time there coaching the basketball and baseball teams at the Catholic elementary school which I attended as a child, I have not spent very much time in Putnam in quite a long while.

This past Fall, however, I felt this yearning to get in my car and go back to this place known popularly by the term *"The Quiet Corner"*. [28] This "nostalgia tour" of mine included eating at a restaurant which was a former local convenience store which I frequented virtually every day when I was growing up. It was the place where I bought ice cream and other treats in the many years I attended the Catholic school which had been located right across the street. It was there where I picked up the daily bus that led me to the high school I attended in a nearby town. [29]That Catholic elementary school of mine was now empty, as was the convent where most of my teachers, nuns who belonged to the Daughters of the Holy Spirit[30], lived, the place where I first learned to play a musical instrument with one of the nuns as my VERY patient instructor!

27 This is from his song which is entitled *My Little Town*.
28 This is a phrase that has been created to identify towns in Northeastern Connecticut.
29 Marianapolis Preparatory School, Thompson, Connecticut.
30 This is a religious community of sisters.

On that same day, I was all excited that I could spend time as well on two local golf courses which I loved to play throughout the years of my youth.[31]

Now, by the time you are reading this book, I will have turned seventy years old.[32] With this reality hovering over me, I am also quite aware that as one grows older, certain nostalgic yearnings tend to emerge within. That is a reasonably well expected part of experiencing one's advancing age. Such is what I feel when I return to my childhood home. Any visit there brings with it a bevy of mixed emotions, for sure. These might include the experience one has when he or she finds oneself reliving joyful moments from days well in the past. Conversely, a visit could deepen a person's awareness that so many of the people who had been so integral to one's life were simply no longer there. In fact, they were no longer inhabiting this earth at all! In those occasional times when I go back, I find so many of these emotions coming to the surface.

On that particularly beautiful Fall Day, I could not help but visualize the experiences of those days gone by. Every time I go back to Putnam. I find those experiences coming to the surface. I can't help but remember them and in my mind's eye I find myself actually picturing all of those hours I spent in that church across the street from Henry's Corner Store, with all of those cars parked in that neighborhood come each Sunday morning as their drivers and passengers packed the pews of the church. Inevitably, I would find myself calling to mind those bitterly cold days when I waited for the bus that took me to my high school as well as the many mornings when I engaged in all kinds of banter about politics and the Red Sox with the people who frequented that store each and every day as they had a cup or two of coffee before they went off to a hectic day at work.

This was the place when I walked in one morning in 1976 and showed off my brand new political button to the owner, a

---

31 These are the Woodstock and Harrisville golf courses!
32 There is something unique about turning 70!

wonderful man named Henry! [33] When he saw my green Jimmy Carter button on my jacket, he just shook his head and smiled. He was quite used to me backing candidates who happened to never win. This time turned out to be different and the nation ended up being led by an excellent President and a wonderful man! [34]

In addition to those years spent in a Catholic school across the street from Henry's Store, as I grew past those early grammar school [35]days, I also spent a lot of time hanging out with Catholic nuns as from the ages of 9 to 17, I served as an altar boy for a large number of sisters who resided at a place called the Provincial House, the national headquarters of a religious order known as the Daughters of the Holy Spirit. These sisters oversaw my parish school and also staffed a high school for girls that my mother had attended back in the 1940's. [36]

My hometown was predominantly Roman Catholic. For those of us raised in what was known back then to many as *"the one, true faith"*, [37]we had little knowledge of those other buildings in town that went by the name of church. As for me, my life growing up Catholic was centered in a very small town with a small geographical area within it where I could quite readily walk or take my bike to my school, church, or the national headquarters of nuns whom I would serve as an altar boy from 1962 until I went off to college in the early 1970's.[38]

In my experience as a child and a developing adolescent, the center of my religious faith was my Catholicism. You will definitely see this reality throughout this book! Yet, as I grew older and

---

33 Henry Girard. May he rest in peace!
34 This was in 1976 when Jimmy Carter was elected to the Presidency.
35 At St, Mary's School, which I attended from 1st to 8th grade.
36 Putnam Catholic Academy, which is now closed.
37 This is a phrase that is often cited by Roman Catholics.
38 Even in the latter days of my high school life, I would be called upon to help with special ceremonies at this national headquarters, best known as the Provincial House. It also housed Putnam Catholic Academy prior to the construction of a new building for that school in the 1960's. My mother was a student there in the 1930's.

began to take an interest in studying religion, I was also fascinated by the different Christian religious alternatives that were available in this town as well. I was intrigued by the presence of the Jewish synagogue in town which was visibly noticeable on the banks of the Quinebaug River, across the street from the Provincial House which I served as an altar boy and where so many of the nuns spent so much of their time. It was there where sisters from that religious community from all over the world would come to visit and to participate in special observances and programs throughout the year. It was also the site of many funerals of the nuns who were part of this religious community and at which I served as an altar boy. Those funerals had a very special impact on me as I was quite cognizant of the commitment of these nuns, whom my mother knew so very well and whom I came to know by seeing them in this building over the years and also because of my mom's long standing connection to them herself! [39]

As my teenage years rolled along, this fascination with "things religious"[40] led to my spending a good deal of time visiting these other churches in town and setting up appointments to talk with their pastors. In retrospect, I wish now that I had taken the opportunity then to visit that synagogue. However, I am pleased that while I was in college, I did visit some Jewish houses of worship, and that I had the opportunity to get a more up close experience of the spirituality to be found in Judaism. These experiences influenced me to always be sure to stress the significance of Jewish faith in the educational programs I led and the sermons I would preach.

Back then, I longed to find out more about the differences between Protestantism and Catholicism and, at that young age, I would spend summer nights and many Sunday mornings going to worship at places such as the local Methodist church, the Episco-

---

39 My mother had cousins who were nuns and was influenced greatly because of her own experience as a child at St. Mary's School and a teenager at Putnam Catholic Academy.

40 An interesting phrase, for sure! It leads to the broader question of how one might define religion!

pal Church where the priest offered great programs for teenagers, the Assemblies of God congregation, where I learned an awful lot about an expression of Christianity about which I knew very little, and the Baptist church right down the street from where I lived, a church building where a Catholic would enter very rarely.

I say all of this without the intention of writing this book as an autobiography. In fact, you can find much more in depth background in a book I wrote years ago deliberately titled "*Crossing the Street*".[41] Instead I am providing you an overview of " the way things were" in my young life in my little home town as a way of comparing that unique period of personal development with what is happening now in the world of religion as we live fully immersed in this new century, far removed, as am I, from those days of my youth!

As I mention at this chapter's beginning, occasionally, I like to go back to Putnam. As I very much enjoy playing golf, I took a ride up there this past summer to play on a couple of golf courses I would often frequent as a child and a teenager. In addition, my former Principal when I worked at a public high school was then serving as the Superintendent of the Putnam schools.[42] He is a man for whom I enjoyed and appreciated working and I looked forward to dropping in and spending some time with him whenever I got into town.

Whenever I go back to the town of my childhood and adolescence, it is inevitable that I will drive around and cover most of the territory in this town where I grew up. I go by my old house, the fields where I played and later coached baseball, [43]that corner

---

41 Published by Energion Publications with a new second edition released in 2022. This book goes into some detail about an interesting experience I had in that Baptist church I mention here. This experience provides the background for that book's title.

42 Daniel P. Sullivan, my principal for several years when I worked as a Counselor in a public high school in South Windsor, Connecticut. He is currently Superintendent of Schools in Colchester, Connecticut.

43 I was the coach of the St. Mary's School baseball team in 1976, 1977 and 1978. In addition, I was also very much involved in coaching in the local

store to which I referred and the old Catholic elementary school I attended which now remains empty with its now tattered and broken down schoolyard in which I and my friends played for 180 days each school year.

That schoolyard is still there, just sitting in the same place, a place that was once full of action, excitement and outright fun, day in and day out. In addition, no visit to Putnam would be complete without driving by or through the property of the building which once was the Provincial House of the Daughters of the Holy Spirit and which now houses a relatively new private school, a school without religious affiliation.[44] In my driving, a lot of memories come back and way up on their list are those experiences which I had in places that had been deliberately established for the purpose of providing opportunities for people to live out their religious faith.

When I go back to Putnam now and I find myself caught up in nostalgia, especially with respect to the religion that undergirded my youth, I am struck by how much has changed:

- As I mention above the Provincial House, which provided training for those sisters and a long career as an altar boy for me, no longer exists. It has been taken over by a new, for-profit college preparatory school, which has developed an incredible national reputation in basketball. [45]
- The national headquarters of the nuns who meant so much in my young life has been moved away from the building which had been teeming with large numbers in those days of my youth and is now housed in a little office setting on the edge of town. [46] I find myself shaking my head nostalgically these days when I drive by the old Provincial House only to see the sign for *Putnam Science Academy!*

Little League program.

44 Putnam Science Academy.

45 See above.

46 It is quite the different setting from that large Provincial House which overlooked my hometown for many years!

Very few sisters remain in the area. However, from what I have been able to tell, the outstanding values that have been part of the life of this community remain and are expressed beautifully in the lives of many lay persons who are connected deeply to the ministry of this wonderful community. [47] I was really thrilled to discover that, though structured differently from that time when both my mother and I were young, this community of faith continues to live on and do good!

- As I allude to above, If one were to walk down the street from my boyhood home, one would soon find my old Catholic school [48] which is now closed, the convent near it completely vacated and the church which once offered many Masses each weekend and whose priests resided in a rectory on the church's property and the place where my mother worked for several years,[49] now relegated to only a Mass or two on the weekends and a building close to empty.
- A drive through town for me would include both seeing some churches which I knew as a child along with new non-denominational faith communities which were not around back then and whose names are quite different from those mainline church names from back in the day.
- Gone are some buildings that were centered on religious faith and that meant so much to the people of my little town, including that wonderful Episcopal Church whose priest I respected greatly[50] and where I loved to visit and to experience both its liturgy and its vibrant programs for youth.

---

47 The Daughters of the Holy Spirit have established a lay apostolate wherein those committed to the values of this religious order play an important part.

48 St. Mary's School.

49 My mother served as a secretary to the church.

50 A young priest, the late Father Paulsen, who was very committed to youth ministry. He was a true inspiration! To be honest, I do not remember his first name. He was not in Putnam for very long and when he left, I was never in touch with him again. Nevertheless, he had a

THE REALITY OF DECLINE

There really is nothing terribly new or unique about what I have witnessed in my return to my roots and my observations concerning the religious foundations of my youth. What has happened in my beloved little town is indicative of what has taken place nationwide and worldwide as well! In fact, the data indicates that we in the United States, while definitely experiencing church decline, have not done so at the pace to be found in other places. [51]

However, the decline IS real and is expressed in many concrete ways :

- Closures of mainline Christian denominations have been increasingly common over these last few years.
- Churches that were once united communities of faith have found themselves divided as a result of different interpretations of theology, Scripture and ethics. Examples include both the Episcopal and Methodist churches. The result is a significant decline in the overall number of churches maintaining their status in either the United Methodist or Episcopal Church. [52]
- Many people within these denominations, as well as others, have switched out of them as these established churches have taken on a pro gay rights agenda. This is seen specifically in the split now found within Methodism and the break found within churches rooted in Anglicanism. Sadly, this has been going on for years among many who used to be connected to the Episcopal Church.
- Many mainline churches are hanging on by a thread and are not investing in programs that were integral to their ministries not that long ago. This includes active Youth Ministry as well as ongoing Adult Education.

---

great impact upon my religious faith at a time when I was doing a lot of exploration!

51 The classic example of this is the religious life to be found in Europe.

52 There have been significant splits in both church communities over these last few years.

- The number of people affiliated with Protestant and Catholic churches has dropped by 26% over these past few years. [53]
- There has been an uptick of 2 to 4 percent in the United States of those who call themselves atheists.
- There have been significant declines in numbers among those who identify with the three traditional groups of Protestants, Orthodox and Catholics.
- There has been an overall 12% decline among those who identify as Christians. [54]

Some Other Important Facts...

It is important that we explore that which is well known as *Evangelical Christianity.* You will read more about my concerns with this expression of Christian faith as we move through this book. Here are some facts about it of which we really need to be aware to get a sense of much of what is happening in the current experience of Christianity in the United States:

- 25% of Christians identify as evangelicals. [55]
- While there has been a slight dip in evangelical churches, it does not match the decline found in the mainline churches.
- There is higher attrition from organized religion among those who are the products of higher education.
- Half of all evangelicals live in the South, traditionally known as *'The Bible Belt'*.
- Interestingly enough, much of the evangelical movement has also been connected with support for politicians who

---

53 These are the most recent statistics at the time of this writing. This is from a Gallup Poll published in 2019 which examines the decline in church membership over the last twenty years.
54 See previous footnote.
55 These individuals would be connected to church congregations which approach preaching and worship with a focus on an evangelical style. This is most evident in its preaching.

would be considered to be "right wing".[56] The best known current example is former President Donald Trump. However, many other very conservative politicians have received much acclaim from voters connected with evangelical churches. Some have taken on an allegiance to a form of Christianity which is far removed not only from the mainline institutional churches' views but also is expressive of a rather troubling extremism which, in my view, does no justice to the teachings of Jesus.

- As a rule, evangelical Christian churches focus on the inerrancy of Biblical texts and engage in an approach to Bible study which focuses in on literal readings of many Biblical stories and specific principles found in many of these stories.

Some very significant concerns...

If one were to take a ride along the streets of a large number of towns in the United States, here is what one would most likely find:

- Vacated church buildings
- Churches that used to be affiliated with a particular denomination that are now closed
- New, independent conservative evangelical churches that have popped up in many of America' s cities or towns
- In fairness, all of this pales in comparison with the European experience which includes a decline in Christians on the European continent from 66% in 1910 to only 26% one hundred years later.

While one might not notice this in driving by, were one to visit a sampling of evangelical churches in most cities and towns,

---

56 This would include many members of the Republican Party. Note: While embracing conservatism for many years, the Republican Party I knew growing up also included something of a broad range of viewpoints, including members and elected officials who identified as moderate or liberal. Such is no longer the case!

an individual would find the active presence of Bible studies as integral to what they offer. The dearth of good up to date Bible study in mainline congregations stands out in comparison to this. Unfortunately, congregations with the most active Bible studies are not to be found in mainline churches but rather in the "evangelical" ones. What is unfortunate in these churches is the process of HOW the Bible is both read and interpreted.[57]

Addressing the concerns....

In the next chapter, it is my intention to address many of the concerns to which I allude above. In addressing them, I will be making specific suggestions and will be referring to programs that have been abandoned by many mainline churches. In suggesting a renewal of these programs, I do not necessarily mean that churches need to do things *"the way things used to be."* Instead, I try to identify ways in which we have gotten away from things that really worked and were very effective within local congregations. This is not to say that I am encouraging a duplication of the past. To the contrary, I advocate for reflecting on programs and approaches that once worked and applying the insights garnered there to the contemporary reality of church life.

More about this in the chapters ahead...

---

57 Evangelical churches hold to a more literal understanding of the Bible than one would find within mainline churches.

2

A Clear and Present Danger

There has always been division in the field of religion. When I was a young man, I grew up in a town that was predominantly Roman Catholic. While there were other churches in town that had been around for quite a few years, their attendance came nowhere near matching that at the Roman Catholic church of St. Mary's. In fact, in addition to the large, impressive church building which housed its worshipers, the parish also supported a rather large school for children from kindergarten to eighth grade, [58]the school which I attended for many years.

For young Catholics growing up in that culture, there was a sense that ours was *"the one, true church"* [59] as that idea had been planted in our minds by the nuns who taught us and from many of the Catholic parents responsible for raising us. Nonetheless, while there was definite religious division in my little town, much of it attributable to the influx of French Canadian Catholics who came to work in Eastern Connecticut's mills, there was a Protestant presence there as well, albeit it was quite small in comparison to the dominant Catholic culture. A trip to the Catholic cemetery, predominantly serving as a resting place for many French-Canadian Catholics, is noteworthy for its earliest tombstones which bear witness to the lives of many Irish Catholics who were present in

---

58 St. Mary's School in Putnam, Connecticut.

59 This is a traditional Catholic understanding of church, an understanding to which I was well exposed as a child!

this town before people came down from Canada to find jobs in the flourishing Northeastern Connecticut mills.

While we were taught both in our school and in many of our homes that the ideal faith passed down from the apostles was Catholicism, there was also an awareness within us that there were other churches in town which people actually attended on Sunday mornings. In comparison with the large building known as St. Mary's, there was a Baptist church right down the road from where I lived as well as Congregational, Episcopal and Methodist churches in and around the downtown area. There was even a converted house not far from the public elementary school that housed an Assemblies of God congregation. There was a notable difference in the size of those buildings compared to that of the Catholic church we attended as well as in the relatively small number of services held on a given weekend, especially in comparison to the number of Sunday and eventually Saturday evening services held at our Catholic church.[60]

In my little town, there were political differences as well among those who frequented certain churches. While there were some Protestant Democrats in town, the preponderance of worshipers in these Protestant congregations leaned toward the Republican party. At the time I was growing up, it was the Democratic Party that controlled the government in Putnam.[61] My father was an example of this connection between church and political party as he both belonged to St. Mary's Church and spent years as a Democratic member of the City Council.

Nonetheless, despite the differences, there was something of a quiet acceptance between Protestants and Catholics, as well as Democrats and Republicans, in those days. In a way, one could call this a sense of respect, though the Catholic expression of Christianity back then most certainly included a deeply rooted sense of the

---

60 St. Mary's Church, Putnam, as noted above.
61 It was also the hometown of Connecticut's well-known Governor, John Dempsey.

Catholic " one, true church." [62] This understanding of church was extremely important to those of us raised as Catholics!

This respect to which I allude was exemplified in many ways; the most well-known to me was an example that involved my mother. My mom worked for many years for the Connecticut Labor Department. Within her office there were two men, both her supervisors, whom she respected very much. One happened to be a loyal deacon in Putnam's Congregational Church and the other was very active at the Lutheran Church in North Grosvenordale, a village in the nearby town of Thompson. [63]

Why am I going into detail about these early experiences of organized religion in my life?

Well, the answer is quite simple…

In looking back upon those days of my youth, I think it is fair to say that there was something of a mutual acceptance of other peoples' religious faith. Now, I am not naïve enough to say that it was either a perfect or ideal acceptance, but, as exemplified in the relationships with others that both my mother and father had, it does make sense to acknowledge a basic level of acceptance which was present within these relationships. This is not to say that Catholic parents would not be upset should their adolescent child talk about leaving the Catholic church or if their Protestant child fell in love with a Catholic and scheduled a wedding in their soon to be spouse's Catholic church. However, it is to state that there was a common understanding prevalent within our society and quite present where I grew up. This understanding included a general recognition of the presence AND the importance of religion within the public sphere.

On some level, though Protestants might be critical of Catholics or vice versa, there was this sense of commonality even amidst the differences! There was an interesting recognition of perceived religious importance which would be found in Catholics who would

---

62 A popular Catholic phrase.
63 This is the town where my father grew up. This is located just outside of Putnam in Northeastern Connecticut.

say of Protestants *"Well, at least they go to church."* [64] This style of acceptance was expressed by Protestants as well! This has been cited by academic scholars within the context of the term *"American Civil Religion."* [65] In short, this phrase pointed to the common importance of religion as part of the functioning of the United States. This was a popular area of study during my college days as a Religious Studies major and it spoke to the religious environment in places such as my hometown of Putnam, Connecticut.

Here is a definition of it:

> *Civil religion, also referred to as a civic religion, is the implicit religious values of a nation, as expressed through public symbols (such as the national flag), and ceremonies on sacred days and at sacred places (such as monuments, battlefields, or national cemeteries). It is distinct from churches, although church officials and ceremonies are sometimes incorporated into the practice of civil religion. Countries described as having a civil religion include France, the former Soviet Union, and the United States.* [66]

FAST FORWARD TO THE PRESENT ...

Now, a few decades removed from that period not so long ago, a different reality has taken its place:

- In Putnam, as in many other towns, the local Episcopal Church has closed.
- The Lutheran church in Brooklyn, not far down the road from where I grew up, closed a few years back as have a good number of other New England churches in Connecticut and nearby

---

64 I heard this many times as I was growing up!
65 See quotation below.
66 This definition is an edited version drawn from a Wikipedia entry. I selected it as a good, clear example of what the phrase means in practical terms.

Massachusetts which were part of the Evangelical Lutheran Church in America.

• Since my childhood years, all kinds of new churches have popped up in Putnam and its nearby surroundings. These churches are not connected to what is known as Protestant mainline denominations yet rather have forged their own relatively new and unique paths in current church activity. In Putnam these days, we see churches that were not around when I was a kid. These are congregations that go by names such as Crossway Church, Hope Community Church, Green Valley Crossing,[67] as well as new, large evangelical churches over the town line in Thompson.

• This all became most apparent to me one day when I played in the golf tournament sponsored by the Catholic prep school which I had attended. [68] On the morning of that tournament, I was paired up to play golf with a fellow alumnus who was actively involved in alumni events. As I was playing golf with him, he told me all kinds of stories regarding his activities as part of a church just a few miles down the road from the high school we both attended. That high school happened to have been established by a rather conservative, traditional group of Catholic priests, many of whom were our teachers. [69] Though he was a loyal supporter of this Roman Catholic school, he was also fully immersed in the experience of evangelical, conservative Protestant Christianity.

Back when I attended that school, very few people attended who happened to be Protestant. It was most definitely a Roman Catholic environment. Now, many decades later, there has been

---

67 This is quite different from the traditional names that are found in most mainline churches. Examples of this might include First Congregational Church, Grace Lutheran Church, All Saints Episcopal Church and many more.

68 This was the annual tournament sponsored by Marianapolis Prep School in Thompson, Connecticut.

69 The Marian Fathers.

much more diversity in this student body, including what is present in this example above, i.e someone who attended a rather conservative Catholic secondary school who eventually would move into a relatively new contemporary evangelical church.[70] At the same time, this person was also involved deeply in his support of this Catholic school. I have discovered that this movement away from the Catholicism of one's youth and often in the direction of "Evangelical Christianity" [71] is not atypical in the lives of many Catholics of my generation.

A CHASM IN CHRISTIANITY

It is really important that we make clear the significant differences present these days between the Protestant mainline, Roman Catholic and Orthodox churches of this time period AND the evangelical Christian churches that have popped up even in places such as Putnam and Thompson, Connecticut, former bastions of Catholicism as well as of strong mainline Protestant congregations. These are relatively new churches that have led people into a unique approach to Christianity which carries along with it a significant number of problematic issues.

Yet before I delve into my rather significant concerns about these "evangelical alternative churches", I need to give them some credit where credit is due:

- These churches tend to emphasize community. People are encouraged to go out of their way to welcome newcomers and make connections with other people in their congregation.
- These churches provide more than an "in and out" Sunday morning experience. They tend to be very active in promoting programs for youth and people of varied ages and backgrounds

---

70 Note: I would describe my Catholic prep school as conservative when considering the influence of the Marian Fathers in the teaching of religion. In contrast, I found many of the lay persons who were my teachers to be on the more liberal side!

71 A more conservative approach with a central focus on the Bible.

within the church. They offer structured Bible studies and are also quite exemplary in staying in touch with members of the congregation who are going through times of difficulty.

- In addition, they have good local reputations for providing food for needy families and needed supplies for children in their local settings. In many of them, there is also outreach beyond the boundaries of where they live and they engage in reaching out to the needy in other parts of their country and the great wide world.

- These congregations also tend to offer a variety of programs both for young people and adults which keep people connected to their church community throughout the course of each week. Generally speaking, they do not espouse the approach of "Sunday morning, in and out."

Contrast what I have described above with what we find in many "mainline" Christian churches, as well as Roman Catholic ones. This is what we will see quite often in many these churches:

- People attend Mass on Sundays and Holy Days.
- Some worshipers proceed to coffee hour after the service. In many churches, people get out of the parking lot as soon as possible.
- There are no adult education programs for adults.
- There is limited social outreach in their activities.
- Once kids are confirmed, the church does not offer them good, worthwhile youth group opportunities. In fact, it is not all together unusual for parents to say that once their kids have been confirmed, they have done their job!

I could go on with even more examples...

HOWEVER — AND THIS IS A PROBLEM...

However, at the same time, it is not unusual for young people and their parents to make note of the fact that some of these other "non mainline or Catholic" churches in the area offer opportunities that are quite appealing! In some cases, young people are drawn to activities at these more conservative, evangelical types of churches because of how positively their friends feel about them and the very fact that they are invited by those friends. On the plus side, once again, these churches:

- Foster a sense of community among the youth
- Help young people experience what they see as offering help to others in need
- Tend to invest energy into children's and youth ministry

While one cannot help but affirm the fact that what I mention above are some very good things, it is important to make note of the significant downside to be found in these churches which maintain an evangelical, conservative, so- called " Bible based" view of Christianity. Here are some of my concerns about those churches:

- In them, young people and adults tend to be taught a literal interpretation of the Bible.
- This interpretation is problematic because the Bible contains a good number of passages which have been cited as "clobber texts", i.e. passages which seem to contradict many of the Bible's core teachings. Examples include such passages as these, among many others:
- "Wives be submissive to your husbands" found in Ephesians 5:4
- The sins identified in the story of Sodom and Gomorrah- Genesis 19:1-28
- Cult prostitution – Romans 1:25-37
- Levitical law regarding homosexuality- Leviticus 18: 22 and 20:13

These passages merely scratch the surface of what is contained within the Bible. They include something of a support of male dominance as well as an implied criticism of those who would define themselves as homosexual. In those churches which view the words of the Bible as the "absolute WORD of GOD", this is extremely problematic.

The reality here is simple: Any preacher in one of these evangelical churches who would suggest that everything is the Bible is NOT to be taken literally or that Scripture does not come from God alone would find himself or herself (most likely himself, as these churches tend to support male dominance) in very deep trouble.

In my view, this Biblical literalism coupled with its disregard for the complexity of the Bible and the history behind its many books and different literary genres is extremely problematic. Much of evangelical Christianity is based on a very poor understanding of the literary contents to be found within the Bible. Unfortunately, this can be seen in the versions of Bibles that are used in these evangelical churches and are sold in the bookstores that provide reading materials for those who are part of these conservative Christian churches.

As an example, I wish to cite a Christian bookstore of rather large size which is only seven or eight miles from my home. This bookstore is replete with materials that promote a very literal interpretation of the Bible. This includes both the published Bibles on their shelves and the plethora of books they stock which have been written by evangelical writers.

In this store, you will not find the writings of distinguished theologians and scholars within the broad history of Christianity. You won't see anything written by people such as Paul Tillich, Teilhard de Chardin, Marcus Borg, Karl Rahner, Richard McBrien, Elizabeth Johnson, Richard Rohr, John Shelby Spong, Ilia Delio or others who are renowned scholars and writers. *You certainly won't find this book or any of my others on those shelves either!*

What you WILL find is what I describe above:

This includes reading materials centered on a literal, non-scholarly interpretation of the Bible and Christian faith. [72] While

---

72 In fairness it should be noted that those who own and support these
    bookstores would argue against my position that they do not provide

evangelical leaders would contend that their seminaries offer the very best in Biblical study, I would definitely challenge their assertion. Some of the finest theologians have been found in these mainline seminaries whose works are either ignored or criticized by those teaching in evangelical settings. [73]

To be as direct as I possibly can be, I contend that we cannot get around the fact there is a division within Christian churches. The statistical data makes quite clear that the more " progressive" churches tend to include many members who have a strong educational background whereas these evangelical churches tend to have appeal to those whose educational background is not quite as full. In saying this, I experience a certain discomfort because I do NOT BELIEVE that one must have a strong undergraduate or graduate school background to be a follower of Jesus. I worry as well about the built in elitism to be found in those who espouse a more "progressive" form of Christianity.

However, at the same time, I must acknowledge that those who sit in churches and listen to pastors whose understanding of the Bible does not include an awareness of the Bible as literature and is not pure dictation from God are at a great disadvantage in their understanding of the Bible.

To be clear, there are also exceptionally well educated, conservative preachers as well as good seminaries and religious institutions which promote an understanding of the Bible based on solid research. However, the reality is that I would nonetheless find myself questioning many of the interpretations that their scholars would give to their research. [74]

---

materials written by "distinguished theologians and scholars". I would contend that much of their Biblical interpretation is simply NOT based on available Biblical scholarship. The tendency is to offer quotations and sayings that provide limited background knowledge of the Biblical text and its context.

73 It should be noted that over the last few years there has been a decline in mainline seminaries in additions to some mergers and closures.

74 I have researched what is contained in many of the books found in "evangelical" bookstores and am quite convinced that the quality of their

I would also caution that many evangelical preachers have been trained at schools that do not offer the best in overall Biblical research.

Yet even more troubling to me is this: These evangelical churches which are quite present in the South yet also to be found all over the United States, including my native area of New England, have included pastors and congregants who somehow have felt a great degree of comfort in supporting the candidacy of so called conservative politicians who have espoused positions that strike me as quite contrary to the spirit of Christianity.[75] This is something we have witnessed in the emergence of Donald Trump as a candidate for the Presidency.

To be even more specific, it troubles me how certain politicians such as Marjorie Taylor Greene, Lauren Boebert, Ted Cruz, Michael Flynn and Jim Jordan, as well as many more [76], feel so comfortable identifying the Gospel of Jesus with a blatant disregard for the needs of the poor, for basic human respect for others and for the policies and behavior in the politician to whom they have virtually pledged their fealty. Yes, I am talking about Donald Trump, the twice impeached former President.[77] At the time of this writing, many gatherings have been held by President Trump's supporters which center on what I see as a very dangerous Christian nationalism. [78]

It simply disgusts me that so many who identify as Christians have at the very same time espoused his Presidency and at the time of this writing are gearing themselves up to support him in yet

---

Bible study and analysis is questionable.

75 I am thinking of positions taken by such elected officials as Senator Ted Cruz, Senator Josh Hawley and Senator Ron Johnson, among many.

76 Unfortunately, at the time of this writing, there are many more in our current Congress.

77 Donald Trump has been very active in promoting his candidacy among those of the Religious Right. This has been quite apparent in the decisions he has made regarding nominating Supreme Court justices as well as other nominees.

78 Michael Flynn has been a leader in this movement.

another run for the highest office in the land, a man who has, in his first term, found himself impeached TWICE! [79]

Did I mention that?...

To be honest, I do not understand how such politicians whom I have named above can justify some of their behavior and attitude toward others. I simply do NOT GET how they see it as in any way connected to the life and the teachings of Jesus!

Nonetheless it is clear: Evangelicalism lends itself comfortably to this approach. I say this realizing that some evangelical leaders DO take a different and healthier approach, one removed from the outright meanness and disregard for the necessity of human kindness found in some of the politicians whom I have identified above!

All of what I describe here stands in contrast to the approach to evangelical Christianity that I respected back in my Catholic days. I am referring to the ministry of Billy Graham.

A JOURNEY BACK TO 1985 ...

In 1985, I was in my seventh year as a religion teacher at a school that went by the name of East Catholic.[80] At that point in my life, I was a Roman Catholic and had not begun a path that would ultimately lead to ordination in the ministry of any church. Among the several classes that I taught was an elective for seniors entitled *Faith for the Young Adult.* Among the many different assignments my students were required to do was a rather unique one as I included in the course requirements a visit to the Hartford Civic Center to witness a Billy Graham crusade.

Now, as we know, Billy Graham was a Protestant evangelical preacher who for many years traveled both in this country and throughout the wider world. Though he was a Protestant, his approach to Christian faith did not hold Catholics in bad standing. As a matter of fact, in one of his rallies in New England years prior, Dr. Graham welcomed the Roman Catholic Cardinal of the Archdio-

---

79 It is rather amazing...and troubling!
80 East Catholic High School, Manchester, Connecticut.

cese of Boston up to the stage.[81] Dr. Graham's approach was rather straightforward. In his view, the core of religious faith for those of us of any church or denomination who would identify as Christians was this: "*Could you acknowledge Jesus as your "personal Lord and Savior"?* [82] I was quite comfortable walking up and affirming that at the "altar call" which was part of his rally. Whether I would do that in the rallies held by modern day evangelists makes for an entirely different story indeed!

So, despite his evangelical Protestantism, Billy Graham had an appeal to Catholics. As a matter of fact, my Dad, who was a born and bred Roman Catholic, used to love those weeks when the Billy Graham crusade filled our television screen every night. Truth be told, so did I.

I mention all of this for one simple reason:

In the Hartford Civic Center where I took my students that evening, there was a certain unity. It was a common understanding those in attendance shared. It was the premise that embracing the teachings and the actions of this man Jesus would provide a worthwhile focus for how we lived out our lives. This affirmation also included a certain simplicity which would often get lost in the world of theology. [83] This simplicity was centered on Dr. Graham's call to those of varied denominational persuasions or none at all to take Jesus into our hearts and to try our best to live as He taught.

His mantra was simple, as I have mentioned above:

Will you accept Jesus as your personal Lord and Savior?

IN THE YEARS THAT FOLLOWED ...

If we were to fast forward a couple of decades and take an close look at the current state of evangelical Christianity, it is clear that we would find ourselves far removed from the simple message Dr.

---

81 Richard Cardinal Cushing, who also had very close ties to the Kennedy family. In 1963, Cardinal Cushing presided at the funeral of President John F. Kennedy and at his burial as well.

82 A favorite phrase at the Graham rallies!

83 The study and discussion of theology can get complicated, for sure!

Graham offered on our TV screens and shared with my students and with me at an arena in Hartford, Connecticut in 1985!

While in those days, Dr. Graham espoused a sense of Christian unity, i.e. Protestants, Catholics, Orthodox and new believers could ALL find unity in a simple acceptance of the teachings of Jesus, the current religious context within the United States, for certain, as well as other parts of the world, embraces a simple fundamentalism which has somehow found itself coupled with a very right wing approach to political decision making.

Now, don't get me wrong: Billy Graham, wonderful as he was, most definitely had an affinity for conservative politics. He was very close to Republican politicians and Presidents such as Richard Nixon. His embrace of these politicians was a definite obstacle as Dr. Graham embraced a conservative politics that, in my view, stood in the way of necessary social change. Over time, I came to discover that.

HOWEVER, his evangelical outreach was far superior to much of what we are seeing today, especially in the ways certain politicians have embraced an evangelical Christianity centered on extreme right wing politics. Without a doubt, it was way superior to that promulgated by his son. [84]

We can recognize this difference in the quotation from Billy Graham which has made its way to many Facebook pages:

> *"I don't want to see religious bigotry in any form. It would disturb me if there was a wedding between the religious fundamentalists and the political Right. The hard Right has no interest in religion except to manipulate it"* [85]

Earlier in this book, I alluded to some of these politicians I have mentioned above. To that list, I would also add many members of Congress, including among them many supporters of that twice impeached former President, Donald Trump. In fact, can-

---

84 Franklin Graham, a well-known evangelical preacher. I find the positions that he takes to be very troubling, as is his justification for many of the actions of former President Donald Trump!

85 A quotation from Dr. Graham as published in Parade magazine in 1981.

didate Trump found a very crafty way to align himself with this evangelical Christianity as a means to garner votes in his Presidential campaigns. As he sought the Presidency, he curried favor with a wide variety of evangelical leaders, including among them the son of Jerry Falwell, who was President of Liberty University prior to his resignation in disgrace, and none other than Billy Graham's son Franklin, a man about whom I have often said: *"He is NO Billy Graham!"*

As I am in the process of finalizing my review of what I have written in this book, the United States has once again been confronted with the reality of yet another school shooting.[86] I am again appalled at the reaction of several elected officials who continue to defend gun rights while at the same time gladly espousing their Christian faith. For the life of me, I cannot make peace with this inconsistency!

Actually, what has happened is that we have seen a significant, intense division within Christian faith, a division between mainline Christians and those of an evangelical, often fundamentalist persuasion. Incredibly as well, many conservative Roman Catholics have also engaged in alliances with conservative evangelical Republicans and have expressed either subtle or direct criticisms of Pope Francis, whom they would see as being "too liberal."

One of my active Youth Group members from my days serving in a Catholic parish has been a very strong advocate for conservative Catholic causes and has been extremely critical of many of the positions held by liberal Protestants as well as many supporters of the ministry of Pope Francis. Interestingly enough, he has forged significant alliances with groups representing the evangelical wing of Protestantism, even to the point of being recognized as a speaker at some of their recent events. His positions are well stated in a recent article he published regarding a presentation given by a Catholic bishop at Fairfield University, a Jesuit college in Connecticut. [87]

---

86 This book is being finalized at the time of the horrific murders in a school in Nashville, Tennessee.

87 Peter Wolfgang, Director of the Family Institute of Connecticut.

While I do not want to hold Billy Graham up as the ideal religious leader who had all of the answers to every religious question, I DO see in him an approach far healthier than that which we are currently experiencing in our deeply divided American religious landscape!

Some Idealistic Hopes

Though I have deep concerns and find myself quite annoyed (an understatement) about the trends that have emerged within organized Christianity, I nonetheless have hope that things need not be the way they are. I say this even in this time when large numbers of Americans have abandoned organized religion and the practice thereof. While I have not done so (*in fact, I think you could say that I have done the opposite*), I do have a certain degree of sympathy for and understanding of their position. In many ways, institutionalized religion HAS failed and most certainly does not always represent itself well. I give examples of this throughout the book.

In fact, I have a rather great degree of anger when I consider all that has happened within institutionalized, organized religion which has brought us to this point.

It is fair here to ask: What IS this point you are talking about?
Here it is:

- *Large numbers of people of a variety of ages see absolutely NO NEED to participate in a religious institution.*
- *Many are also quite comfortable with not raising their own children in an environment in which they would be participating in a religious institution.*

To be clear, I know a lot of people who take these positions who are incredibly caring, loving spouses, partners, friends, and parents. They have rejected organized religion in practice while, at the same time, are living lives of kindness and service to others.

They are wonderful people! At the risk of being simplistic, they might very well fall into the category of "anonymous Christian." [88]

I want to be straight up about this and make two comments about which I feel very strongly:

- I understand where many of these good, sincere people come from. Organized religion has often failed people. The historical examples are quite far reaching and very clear.
- Nevertheless I still think churches, synagogues, temples and mosques are important.

At the core of these affirmations is my strong conviction that we need a significant revitalization of mainline Christianity. My own definition of this includes the longstanding different branches within the Christian faith. My emphasis would be on the revitalization of Roman Catholic, Orthodox and mainline Protestant churches as well as a renewal in what is offered both within these congregations AND with these congregations moving in the direction of working TOGETHER with one another. This would include joint adult educational programs, shared worship opportunities, vigorous social outreach, and a vibrant ecumenically centered youth ministry!

In addition, at the risk of being considered unreasonably idealistic and living in a dream world, I would make the claim that, as far as humanly possible, it is important to find a way to put a halt to the closures in mainline churches as much as can be done practically. While many would argue that this approach is a trip into a past that cannot be reconstructed. I would respond quite differently. I develop these thoughts of mine later in this book!

I would encourage churches to engage in a healthy self-examination which includes a deep exploration of WHY they exist and

---

88 A phrase popularized by the theologian Karl Rahner. Its underlying premise of this is that even people who have not heard the Christian Gospel may be saved through Jesus Christ. This would be because of how they lived their lives.

what could be the impact of their presence in the contemporary context of this complicated world.

Conversely, I would encourage them to ask a reverse question as well:

Would you consider the ways in which church closures in mainline Christian churches could really HURT the church of the future? Maybe you think it would, maybe not. We will come back to this important question later in this book. Personally speaking, I have some real concerns but, at the very least, we all should be sure to give that question some very serious thought!!

My hope is that as you read through these pages, you might find some suggestions OR develop those of your own in response to that which you have read which might lead to making possible the emergence and the renewal of vibrant Christian churches which can make a positive difference in the years and decades that lie ahead!!

3

THE IMPORTANCE OF YOUTH MINISTRY

Most of us are quite aware of the powerful impact caused by the presence of COVID-19.[89] One could go on at great length about the effect it has had on how we live out our lives. Among the many things I will remember about its early days is something that took place in a church I was serving as pastor at that time.

In early February of 2020, when I was serving at a church in central Connecticut [90], as the result of a conversation I had with the church's musician whom I have known quite well from back in his high school days,[91] I put out an invitation to several Protestant and Catholic churches in the Greater Hartford, Connecticut area inviting their youth to come to our church on a Saturday night in early March and participate in an ecumenical Youth Night [92], an evening that would bring together teenagers from a number of different churches and varied religious traditions for an evening of singing, conversation, shared prayer AND some delicious pizza.

I was exceptionally pleased with the response of those who were committed to youth programming in a good number of local congregations. They were genuinely excited that something like this

---

89   The virus that impacted our nation and our world, beginning in early 2020.

90   Grace Lutheran Church, ELCA, Plainville, Connecticut.

91   Eric Hutchinson.

92   A term used in many churches.

was being done for the youth of these churches. I was also thrilled
with the willingness of adults in our congregation to be of help and
so glad that one of our young adults was interested in providing
music for this occasion. I had come to discover that he was a very
talented young man indeed!

However, this excitement, though certainly warranted, reflected what I found to be a sad reality! In my experience in churches
over the years, I have discovered a distinctive downward trend in
programming for youth. To be more specific, what I am talking
about is the kind of VOLUNTARY options for teenagers that were
part of church congregations for a very long time.[93]

What I am focused on here is NOT Sunday School or Confirmation classes or, as is the case in some traditions, classes to prepare
adolescents for Baptism. Instead, I am referring to local churches
having some kind of structure in place whereby youth can spend
time with other youth and participate in discussions on real life
topics, in worship which is quite personalized and differs from
the traditional worship to which they may be dragged on Sunday
mornings, and which offers opportunity to explore real life issues
in depth as well as to engage in service to others.

My experience has been that, over the years, active, vibrant
youth ministry has, for all intents and purposes, withered away in
local mainline congregations. It tends to remain a vibrant part of
more conservative, evangelical congregations.

I find this reality extremely troubling…

THE WAY WE WERE

In the early 1980's, I pretty much had two full time jobs. Both
involved working in a "religious context" with adolescents. My
everyday job entailed teaching religion classes at a Catholic high
school. As part of that job, at one point I developed a course called
"Christian Leadership" in which students under supervision would

---

93 I am referring to the time of my own youth as well as my experience in
    youth ministry in the 1980's and 1990's, much of which is referred to
    throughout this book.

engage in a variety of activities relevant to living out the core of Christian faith. Among these activities were included specific ones where students would go into local churches and meet with those who were participating in their congregation's youth programs. My students would give presentations in which they would talk about their own life and the place of faith within it and engage in serious conversations with the youth who were there listening to them. This involved a great deal of work on the students' part, yet I was quite thrilled that they were willing to embrace the challenge!

My other job involved serving as a Director of Religious Education at some Roman Catholic churches in central Connecticut and in that capacity overseeing and directing specific programming in the area of youth ministry. [94]

Those were exciting days as youth ministry programs I had served in these churches developed in these different ways:

- There was a voluntary weekly meeting which covered a wide variety of topics of importance to the youth who gathered for it.
- There were youth ministry leadership teams comprised of those who were part of the youth group. This team would help evaluate the programs offered within the church's youth ministry and provide feedback to the adult leaders, including the staff member responsible for supervision of the group.
- There was a focus on offering youth group retreats which were usually held away from the site of the church.[95] These retreats varied in structure and would include programs for all youth connected with that church in any way. That would include young people who were not church goers and/or whose family was not either.

---

94 This included regularly scheduled Sunday night Youth Group meetings as well as a variety of retreat opportunities in locations away from the church building.

95 They were often held at St. Thomas Seminary, Bloomfield, Connecticut, which was once the site for the formation of many priests in the Archdiocese of Hartford.

- There were shared experiences with members of other congregations.
- In addition, there were also required retreats for those going through the church's Confirmation program.

At around the same time, as I note above, I was also working as a teacher in a local Catholic high school. During this time, I suggested a new elective course which was approved by the administration. The title of the course was CHRISTIAN LEADERSHIP and the requirements for those seniors who were enrolled in the course included some of the following:

- There was extensive reading on a variety of religious topics with well-designed classroom presentations and student led discussions on those readings.
- Students would participate as part of a leadership team at retreats these students would offer to youth in local congregations.
- Students would offer presentations on a variety of important topics to other students in this course.
- Students were required to participate in a retreat that centered on the overall dynamics of this course.

Entrance into this class was dependent upon an interview toward the end of the previous academic year.

One of the most memorable activities, as noted above, was that in which many of these students participated in which they would be part of a leadership team that coordinated retreats for students in local parishes.

I would attend these retreats and supervise them in addition to offering some messages to the young people in attendance BUT the core of the retreat centered on the leadership and witness of those who were part of this unique course in the school's Religion department.[96] It was a course that required a lot of extra work and a significant time commitment. In looking back, I am so proud of

---

96   I worked in the Religion Department of this school for ten years.

the work done by my students in this newly developed course in the Catholic high school where I taught.

Several years later, after I had left the Roman Catholic Church and was preparing for ordination in the United Church of Christ,[97] I was most fortunate to have been offered a position at a local Protestant church in which I directed Christian Education programs.[98] As part of my ministry, I was responsible for instituting an active Youth Group. In working with this group, I was so grateful to have had some outstanding volunteer adult leaders and many young people who were actively engaged as they gathered together on Sunday evenings.

An amazing outgrowth from that group was their engagement in offering the play *Godspell* to the wider community. The passion with which these young people participated in and promoted this play which would fill the church's seats for a winter weekend is something I will never forget. Amazingly, this production led to what became an annual event in the life of that church[99] and it forged an incredible bond between youth and adults of all ages. I look back on this time with great joy and I am also thankful that one of the leaders among the youth in these productions has served with me as a musician at a number of churches which I have served as a pastor. [100]

AN HONEST OBSERVATION

To be perfectly honest, my most recent experiences in working at churches and attempting to connect with other local churches to do youth ministry in the areas in which I have served has disap-

---

97 Also known popularly as the UCC.

98 First Congregational Church, UCC, in Vernon, Connecticut.

99 In the years that followed, this church presented an annual youth led musical, including an original entitled *Believer* developed by two of its members, Eric Hutchinson and Michael Sadler. Over the years, this play was also taken to the road in both Connecticut and Massachusetts!

100 Eric R. Hutchinson, current musician at Grace Lutheran Church, ELCA, Plainville, Connecticut, where I was pastor from 2019-2021.

pointed me. The times have changed significantly since those days when I served in youth ministry in churches back in the 1980's.

What I have observed quite sadly is that the energy to form and develop viable, voluntary youth groups both within mainline churches and ecumenically has, for all intents and purposes, faded into the sunset over the course of the last two decades.

My experience has been that many churches, both mainline Protestant and Roman Catholic, offer programs which center on getting young people through the process of Confirmation preparation. While this is important and I support it, I am also troubled by the fact that for many of our youth and their parents, being confirmed as "adult Christians" [101] represents the end of the process of being engaged in religious education. *I would contend that, for most of the adults in mainline congregations, such was the case in their own lives.* Were one to look at adults of my age, one might find good examples of activities that were offered to us. However, in our current context, Confirmation in many churches has come to mark the end of religious education for those who participated in the process of preparing for it.

Whereas youth ministry was a vibrant and vital part of church life in many Catholic and Protestant congregations through the 1960's, 70's and early 80's, in my view, this vibrancy has faded. As I see it, this is extremely problematic.

A GLIMPSE OF HOPE

In late February in the year 2020, while I served as pastor of an ELCA church in Connecticut, I was most fortunate to do so alongside the musician at our church, a talented young man with whom I had stayed in touch over the years and had suggested as the person to hire when the position opened at my then new church. This musician whom I have mentioned above, Eric Hutchinson[102], and I developed a plan to hold a "Youth Night" hosted by our congregation.

---

101 A phrase that has made its way into language used by religious educators.
102 More about him later in this book!

The plan for this evening was to offer structured opportunities for young people from a variety of local churches, both Protestant and Catholic, to come together for an evening in which they would:

- Participate in activities to help meet other youth from different congregations.
- Share in discussions about relevant topics in the lives of young people.
- Enjoy a variety of music led by Eric and other volunteers.
- Eat pizza![103]

In essence, this was really the model upon which I had formulated youth ministry programs back in the 1970's and the 1980's.[104] I found it as simple and effective.

What was MOST INTERESTING was that when I started making contacts and inviting youth groups in the area, I found very few congregations that offered ongoing programs for youth.

HOWEVER, a great thing occurred:

> *Those churches that did show interest in participating had adult leaders who were very enthused to do so. What was wonderful here is that there was an excitement in some churches that someone was suggesting we organize a program for youth. My sense is that those adults had some fond recollections of church youth ministry involvement years ago and continued to see it as a vital part of the church!*

What was wonderful as well was how engaged many adults in our congregation were as were the very small number of youth who were connected to our church. The level of voluntarism among the adults and enthusiasm of our youth was both exciting and uplifting. As a matter of fact, a young adult in our congregation who had excellent musical skills offered to participate in offering

---

103 An integral part of youth activities!!
104 To which I alluded in my previous comments about youth groups!

some music as part of the evening.[105] In addition, a wonderful older couple from within the church offered to help out with the event both by taking care of the necessary pizza and through being present at this event![106]

AND THEN...

As we drew toward the Saturday evening in which this well anticipated event was to take place, an event which had many youth in the area as well as their adult leaders quite excited, something was looming on the horizon. Our world and now our nation was dealing with the emergence of what has come to be known as COVID-19 and schools, businesses, and churches, as well as families, were bracing themselves for the reality that things were going to change VERY quickly.

As we know quite well, they eventually did. Months went by when people were not allowed to gather in church buildings. In person religious education, adult education and youth ministry programs were discontinued. Simple ways of connecting within congregations, which were already in a rather wobbly state in many churches, simply faded away.

When COVID eventually struck, a number of churches DID work very hard to provide opportunities for adults and youth alike to stay connected. A lot of creativity was involved. Great innovative things began happening online. In our congregation, we made sure to arrange programming for Confirmation candidates which were held online, were interactive and included important discussions based on material in relevant resources that were part of this preparation program. As a result, as COVID lifted, we were able to celebrate Confirmation in our sanctuary with a very good attendance which exhibited great support for our youth!

---

105 As neglected as youth ministry programs are in many churches, programming for young adults is as well.
106 Bruce and Sharon Messenger, active and dedicated members of this church.

Nevertheless, as time went on, the opportunities to meet in person began to fade. Despite the explosion in the number of people accessing technology and using the internet, the change in routine within local churches was quite apparent. Not long before the coronavirus hit, one could readily notice, as stated above, a clear decline in youth ministry opportunities for youth in the congregations of mainline Protestant denominations, as well as in the Catholic Church. Quite honestly, it is far too simplistic to just blame the pandemic. It cannot be used as a convenient excuse for inaction! Nonetheless, it most definitely had a considerable impact!

This all made sense in terms of the concurrent reduction in adults who were able to connect with these churches. From my experience, many mainline churches worked hard to provide preparation programs for Confirmation, for sure, while the more voluntary programs for young people remained in the background, at best!

The vibrancy of youth group programming which I was fortunate to experience in the years prior through my involvement coordinating youth ministry within both Catholic and Protestant churches, as well as in coursework in a Catholic high school where I taught [107] was already in danger prior to the emergence of the pandemic. This is important to note as the pandemic could end up all too readily being used as a convenient excuse. Mainline youth ministry WAS in trouble well before COVID-19!

Sadly however, the pandemic's presence dealt a blow from which many churches have not yet recovered. Much of this, one could argue, was unavoidable. Despite the obstacles made manifest in those difficult days of widespread COVID-19, churches nonetheless sought to find ways to insure that teenagers would be able to be confirmed.[108] However, other youth programming was placed on the back burner, similar to how other church programs were at the same time.

---

107 East Catholic High School, Manchester, Connecticut.
108 This remained a priority!.

As I see it, one of the reasons this had occurred was connected to the fact that in many churches, spending an appropriate amount of money to hire someone who would focus on youth ministry was simply not happening because of budgetary concerns made necessary due to the decline in attendance and consequent giving to the church.

Many pastors, busy as they were with trying to keep the congregation afloat during the pandemic, were not inclined to prioritize youth ministry. In fairness, pastors needed to take upon themselves the formulation of new ways to provide worship services, including getting involved with the technology required to do so. These were areas that were not part of church leadership for most pastors prior to the emergence of this pandemic! Speaking as one who served a s pastor during this stretch of time, I would contend that it was a very unique experience, for sure!

COVID-19 AND THE CHURCH...

Over the last couple of years, considerable attention has been made regarding the number of pastors who resigned from their positions at the churches they served during the period in which COVID-19 swept the nation and the world.

While each individual case is unique, I DO think it is fair to say that the pastoral work required during COVID-19 represented a significant shift in strategies and priorities for many pastors. In addition, the political climate surrounding COVID led to considerable tension within some congregations. While I was fortunate that in my own pastoral work, I did not experience that tension, I am well aware of how much pain and anguish it caused for so many church leaders in what was already an extremely difficult time!

During this time of pandemic, pastors needed to find ways to remain in contact with those members who were not connected via the internet. In many situations, this included formulating written materials for people to get in the mail and read at home. It also involved considerable time spent simply having telephone conversations with dedicated church members who were not inclined to 'follow the church on Facebook or Twitter', [109] much less the church's updated web site!

As a result of this pastoral responsibility, my sense is that many pastors may have felt that immersing themselves in coordinating and activating effective youth ministry was one thing too many. This is understandable. However, the result was a decline in voluntary youth ministry activity within the church.

Interestingly enough, young people were the ones who tended to be quite adept at the use of a variety of technological resources. While churches made significant efforts to reach adults with opportunities for worship and religious education, a basic fact is that for many church goers, especially more elderly ones, the use of the Internet was not an integral part of their lives. However, I discovered that by reaching out to youth and engaging them in activities that could be done online, one could maintain something of great value, i.e. the presence of an active, voluntary youth ministry within the church even when this community of faith was dealing with the problems caused by the unwanted and unplanned for presence of COVID!

While offering opportunities for Confirmation was important, an underlying approach was also quite evident. For many years, in both Protestant and Catholic churches, parents took comfort in the reality that if they just got their kids through Confirmation, they were successful in doing their job as parents connected to their church. While the intention was quite good and students were seen as capable of making their own decisions, there was a problem in this approach as well.

While I am sure there was a deep-down intent to respect the freedom of the individual teenager in making the decision to be baptized or confirmed, there was also an implicit sense that if they were to get through this religious education program in their church, these youth could now be freed from having to participate in any future activities geared toward youth in their local con-

---

109 A typical slogan!

gregations. For many parents, this was the selling point in their conversations!

This implicit expectation was fortified through the ways in which churches which once had vibrant youth group programming had, for all intents and purposes, moved away from offering them for young people who had already gone through the Confirmation process. This was made obvious to me during that time when I contacted churches to invite them to join the youth program that I have described above. However, I remained quite pleased with the interest that lay persons showed as expressed in the example I gave as part of this chapter.

Ideally, lay persons working in close relationship with clergy in these congregations most certainly had the potential to keep youth ministry alive in churches, including those that were fairly small in membership. I say this fully cognizant that some would differ with me by contending that there are just not enough kids around and the church should expend time and money in programs outside of youth ministry. I honestly think that for some, youth ministry in the congregation was perceived as something that "used to be" back many years prior but was not easy to get rolling in this particular period of time!

A LOOK BACKWARDS

As I have considered these issues which have been of great concern to me, I have found myself looking backwards to the year 2000. It was during that year when I was serving as Director of Christian Education in a congregation of the United Church of Christ and was not yet ordained that I was part of an experience concerning youth ministry that I will never forget and that has become a reference point for much of what I have done in my years serving as a pastor.

To make a long and memorable story short, in addition to the regular weekly Sunday Night Youth Group meetings, attended by a good number of youth who had ALREADY been confirmed but were coming to these meetings voluntarily, some participants in the group floated the idea of having the church's young people develop and host a production of a musical, specifically the musical Godspell, which had been suggested by a church member and teacher, someone with a great background in the direction of youth musicals. [110]

What was so impressive was that the youth followed through with their plan and enlisted a bevy of their friends to eventually develop a musical that packed the church for an entire weekend and which led to the development of youth sponsored performances in that church over the next several years. Now, the key element involved in BOTH these youth group meetings and the development and implementation of the theatrical projects I mention here is this:

Nothing that these young people did was a REQUIREMENT but instead the impetus to participate in these performances came from within each of them. As a result, in addition to presenting productions that spoke to the lives of those watching, through the process of performing and joining together with their fellow actors they also engaged in significant reflection and shared discussion of the deeply rooted "spiritual" topics contained within the performances of which they were a part!

By the time that I was serving as a youth minister in this church, I had abandoned my membership in the Roman Catholic Church and resigned from my ministry within it as an ordained Permanent Deacon.[111] However, I look back at the years I spent as a youth minister in several Catholic churches, as well as the ministries in which I was engaged while teaching at a Catholic high school and see great similarities between and among them. In each context, there was:

- A tendency among youth toward volunteering for worthwhile causes. In churches I served, I discovered so much enthusiasm in young people there who wanted to go out of their way

110 The late Joseph Connolly.
111 As explained in this book, one of the ordained ministries in the Roman Catholic Church.

to help others. This inevitably evolved into wonderful, often creative ways to do so!

- Word of mouth from friends of the youth which inspired them to participate!
- A sense that this was an integral part of their weekly life, despite their busyness with school and a multiplicity of activities.

The bottom line was simple: These youth were not REQUIRED to participate in any of these things BUT they did and did so because these youth events gave them opportunities to find significant meaning:

- The youth group gatherings provided them with a sense of connection and community.
- Their outreach activities made real for them the importance and practical implications of SERVICE TO OTHERS.

In addition, I need to make clear that even as I immersed myself in youth ministry in Protestant churches, it is important to note that many Roman Catholic parishes and high schools were offering similar opportunities during that time.[112] However, as stated above, I am sad to say that in both Protestantism and Catholicism things have not been quite the same within these past few years!

This is expressed powerfully in a comment by one of my former Catholic school students in the 1980's, now an Attorney in the Commonwealth of Virginia:

> *"Your vision of what a church should be reminds me of what my parish was headed towards in the early 80s in Vernon, Connecticut.[113] Active youth group, close knit community where the priest preached about things we could all understand. That personal touch, by the Catholic church at least, has completely disappeared for me over the past thirty*

---

112 This was the tail end of a period of vibrancy in Youth Ministry within American Catholicism.

113 Sacred Heart Church, Vernon, Connecticut, a vibrant, progressive Roman Catholic church which closed many years ago.

five years. Dogma has supplanted spirituality and ethics to the point where I'm not sure religion is the vehicle to make that happen." [114]

What a powerful statement indeed!

A Strategy for Revitalization of Youth Ministry: Some Practical Suggestions

First and foremost, local churches need to embrace the importance of youth ministry within their congregations. Church Councils and Christian Education leaders need to think seriously about the goals of their programs. As I have noted, much of what constitutes ministry to youth is centered around educational and service programs which prepare one for the celebration of Confirmation or for Baptism in those church traditions that encourage believers' baptism rather than the baptism of infants. [115]

What is interesting is that in the earliest days of the Christian church, that which we now call Confirmation was part of a threefold initiation into the church community centered on a celebration on the night of the Easter Vigil. This recapturing of the importance of this Vigil is something that has become part of Lenten and Easter worship in the Roman Catholic church over these past few decades. [116] Incorporated into that service for adults who have not been baptized is an initiation into church through the celebration of Baptism, Confirmation and Communion. For those teenagers and adults who may have been baptized earlier in their lives, the celebration of Confirmation in which candidates affirm their Baptism takes on considerable significance. Within the Baptist tradition, being baptized is connected to the experience of free choice in the individual.

---

114 Attorney Edward Nuttall
115 This is exemplified in the traditions of Baptist churches.
116 Oftentimes, baptisms are part of the Easter Vigil service and those already baptized share in a public renewal of their Baptismal vows within this service.

While the reality is that Confirmation in and of itself is a meaningful rite, the practical fact remains that, for all intents and purposes, being confirmed is perceived for many young people and those others in their families in the same way as a "secular" graduation would be. Consequently, what we have seen over the course of the years is the reality of a plethora of people who were confirmed sometime between the ages of 15 and 18 who see themselves as no longer needing to participate in educational programs that are part of their church's life. At the same time, a great number of the parents of those students have come to feel that they have "done their job."

SOME PRACTICAL SUGGESTIONS

As I conclude this chapter in which I have expressed great concern about the loss of important youth ministry programs within congregations, I wish to offer some suggestions for congregations to consider. While each church is unique, for sure, it is my hope that these suggestions could be helpful and might be applied within local faith communities:

1. I would suggest that all congregations offer middle and high school students the opportunity to be part of a Youth Group. Ideally, it is best to separate middle school and high school youth groups from one another. However, there may be situations where groups can engage in certain projects together. Nonetheless, it is important that for the most part, youth be separated by age.

2. Participation in a church's Youth Group should NOT be part of required preparation for the reception of Confirmation or Baptism in those churches that do not practice infant Baptism.

3. Even when a congregation has a small number of youth, it should look at asking the questions regarding how they can reach out to young people within their locality. Many churches have ceased to offer youth programming because they do not have enough young people in their congregation. This

can be offset by creative advertising in the local community, including information accessible on the Internet. Even when congregations do not have a large number of young people, I would encourage them to be strong advocates for youth ministry within their communities.

4. It is essential that youth activities are not perceived as a requirement. Instead, I suggest really promoting and talking up the options that are available. I also suggest encouraging youth to pass this information on to their friends, including those not connected to "organized religion."

5. Ideally, it would be good for a church to hire someone whose responsibility would be to serve as an adult leader. Wherever possible, money should be set aside for this. If not possible, relying on volunteers is acceptable provided provision be made for those volunteers to be trained as well as for them to share responsibilities with other volunteers. Taking steps to avoid potential burnout among adults is crucial!

6. Even if a clergyperson is not charged with leading every activity of a youth group or managing every aspect of the group's ministry, he or she should be connected to it and the young people should know that this clergyperson IS involved in the work of this group!

7. Youth Ministry programs within congregations should include the following:

    a. Regular Youth Group meetings… I would suggest twice a month as a reasonable goal.

    b. Outreach to the youth groups of other local churches

    c. Hosting broad based youth programming within their communities at least twice a year. This would involve connection with youth served through agencies in local cities and towns.

    d. Youth assuming leadership positions at worship-reading, sharing their ideas, singing, etc.

e. When youth participate in leading worship, it should be during worship services that are part of the congregation's overall life. I would highly recommend that youth worship NOT be separate from standard, traditional worship within the congregation. Occasional youth worship is fine, for sure, but it is best, in my view, to integrate the ministry and worship of youth within the overall experience of the wider church.

f. Youth Groups should seek out ways to bring in musicians who could help raise money for important causes.[117] Doing this could have the positive impact of showing others about the concern for social outreach exhibited by this church. It also could have the added effect of widening perceptions of what a church is about and what goes on in its building other than official church ceremonies!

g. A recognition and acceptance of the fact that while some young people may not be interested in official religious teachings, there is something about connecting with other youth that is important to them. Consequently, youth groups in churches should be open to those young people who do not "attend church" [118] and/or have doubts about or no background in institutional religion.

h. Ways to insure interaction between youth and other constituencies, including younger children and adults of all ages. As an overall goal, the integration between and among constituencies of different ages within the church is really a necessity.

In forming and developing youth groups, churches need to think outside of the box and not see the development of youth

---

117 During the time period in which I served several congregations, youth were heavily involved in bringing in local young musicians, as well as a variety of singers.

118 These have been wonderful experiences in churches I have served.

ministry as something which only applies to young people who are already connected with this particular congregation. There should be encouragement given to youth in a particular church to INVITE friends who are not connected with this or any other church.

THE ROLE OF THE PASTOR AND/OR OTHER CLERGY

You may find my comments here to be somewhat controversial!

It has been my experience in serving as a pastor in several congregations, that over the past decade or more, mainline churches have been virtually moribund with respect to youth activities. For all intents and purposes, those programs in which I was involved in various churches I served twenty or more years back have fallen by the wayside. While I am not suggesting that it is easy to make a return to the so called "good old days" of youth ministry in the church, I AM suggesting that churches think creatively about the importance of offering good experiences for young people. In order to do so, they need to look beyond the usual ways in which programs are developed for youth and think broadly and realistically.

What is rather clear in looking at the life of adolescents [119] is that a connection to others is very important. This is acted out in a variety of ways. What youth ministry well done can offer young people include:

1. Opportunities to reflect upon life's major questions.
2. Opportunities for positive interaction with other young people
3. An outlet for serving others together with their peers.

What I have found quite troubling is the decline in church efforts to offer youth ministry programming. Over the last few years, including those before the onset of the pandemic, as I stated earlier in this chapter, I was noticing that in my contacts with church leaders in the field of Christian Education, many churches were simply not offering programs for youth. While they were providing classes for Confirmation students, this was pretty much

---

119 This is basic adolescent psychology!

it and programming for youth who had already been confirmed was not part of their overall plan for Christian Education.

There is much that is understandable about and explains this. The reality is that there are not as many parents of potential Confirmation students for whom involvement in church life is an integral part of their overall lives. This is reflected in the declines we see in church attendance.

Back in our parenting days [120], our children's participation in Catholic religious education was something they shared with a great number of their peers whose parents had a Catholic upbringing. Such is not so much the case in these days. What is also noteworthy is the significant decline in weddings held within the church setting or having a clergyperson as their officiant. Down the road (and it has already begun), this has an impact, of course, on the number of youth who are part of a congregation.

In my early years serving as a Permanent Deacon, I discovered that in the church's office there was a list on the bulletin board which provided information regarding the weddings scheduled to be held inside of that church. It was quite the extensive list!

However, as the years went on, the list got smaller and smaller. Couples were opting NOT to get married in formal ceremonies inside of the church building. In many cases, they decided to have their wedding witnessed not by clergy but instead by those empowered as justices of the peace or perhaps by friends or family members who were one-day officiants.[121]

There was a variety of reasons behind this trend. One that really stands out is the simple fact that the connection to the institutional church was simply not part of the life of the couple. Of course, other reasons factor in as well. Given the Roman Catholic position regarding divorce and remarriage, those engaged couples impacted by this would usually opt out of going through the annulment process that is part of Roman Catholic canon law. However, this is not the only reason for the decline in church weddings.

---

120 I am referring to myself and my wife here!
121 See information about this mentioned later in this chapter.

POST CONFIRMATION BREAKAWAY

As noted earlier, there has been a growing tendency in both mainline Protestant and Roman Catholic churches in the direction of young people being engaged only minimally in church participation once they have completed the process of being confirmed. This breakaway has led many young people into a habit which lasts into adulthood. This fact, coupled with such realities as the ages in which youth now get married as well as the possibility of people meeting future partners from places outside of where they grew up, often from different religious backgrounds, has led to a major decline both in weddings within the churches in which they were raised or even in the same geographic area.

In addition, there has also been a new trend involving those who officiate at weddings. Whereas for many, a traditional approach has been to have one's wedding officiated by a clergyperson, what has now developed is the "one day officiant" [122] approach whereby in many states, individuals can actually be commissioned to officiate at the wedding ceremony of a relative or friend on a one day only basis.

Such an approach is quite removed from those days when my wife and I got married. During our first few years as an engaged couple and into our married years, we attended many weddings of family members and friends who were raised within a Christian faith community and whose weddings were celebrated in a church, officiated at by someone ordained, usually a priest.

Years after we were married, the trend continued, though, in the Catholic church, many weddings were performed by ordained deacons, often in marriage ceremonies where a non-Catholic bride or groom would not be able to receive Communion according to Catholic Church canon law. [123] Over time, much of this has evolved into what we see today, i.e. a continuing decline in "religious" wedding ceremonies.

---

122 This is allowed in many states.
123 These are a body of laws binding on Roman Catholics.

Through actions of putting youth ministry on a church's back burner, perhaps as something they wished they could do if only they had a greater number of kids, local churches are really doing a disservice to those who could draw on a healthy, positive youth group experience, one that could make a long-term difference in their lives.

A personal note: I have known a good number of young people whose involvement in youth group during their high school years has continued to make a difference in their adulthood. This has been expressed in different ways.[124]

At the time I am writing this, as you know, I have just turned seventy years old.[125] For all intents and purposes, my time serving as a leader in church youth groups, Protestant or Catholic, is over. However, though I am no longer serving as a pastor in local churches, my interest in the future of the church and the future of meaningful youth ministry, has not waned. For a plethora of reasons, youth ministry within the mainline churches is not what it used to be. Its absence is all too readily accepted while more conservative churches continue to offer programming for their youth within the same communities served by those in the mainline.

In my view, mainline Christianity needs to respond to this troubling reality by raising the need for positive, creative youth ministry programming, placing it high on the agenda of what a local church needs to do as it faces its future. It is a ministry of the church which needs NOT to be ignored!

---

124 Carlos Castillo who currently works on the staff of Hampshire College in Massachusetts , my former student at East Catholic and Youth Group member at St. Bridget's Church in Manchester, Connecticut,, is an excellent example of this!

125 Had I mentioned this before?? LOL!!

4

A FAREWELL TO NOSTALGIA

Come gather 'round people wherever you roam
And admit that the waters around you have grown
And accept it that soon you'll be drenched to the bone
If your time to you is worth saving
Then you better start swimming or you'll sink like a stone
For the times, they are a-changin'.[126]
— *Bob Dylan*

Over the years, I have served in many different churches of varied denominations. Prior to ordination as a Roman Catholic Permanent Deacon, I was a Director of Religious Education and a Youth Minister in several Catholic churches. Upon my ordination, I began serving as a Permanent Deacon in a local Catholic parish not far from where our family lived. [127] When I made the transition into Protestantism, I proceeded to serve in a variety of churches within both the United Church of Christ and the Evangelical Lutheran Church in America.[128]

Throughout these years, I have noticed the evolution of a rather amazing phenomenon. As the years have gone by, it has become clearer each week, that the majority of people attending

---

126 Words and music by Bob Dylan.
127 St. Margaret Mary Church, South Windsor, Connecticut.
128 ELCA.

worship voluntarily within Roman Catholic and mainline Protestant churches are people who are sixty years old or more.

In my time as a pastor, I have been so fortunate and so blessed to have gotten to know many of these older congregants quite well. I have learned from listening to their experiences about how special the unique experience of church has been in their lives. Even when set back by the emergence of the COVID virus that struck the United States beginning in 2020, large numbers of these senior citizens returned to in person worship when the worst days of the pandemic faded away and made going to worship possible.

Some were able to access these worship opportunities online while others were quite grateful for how their churches provided them ways outside of cyberspace to stay in touch. They benefited from worship services sent to them at home and for the messages developed by their pastors and accessible for them through the United States Postal Service! [129]

THE ROAD TO CLOSURE

Prior to the pandemic[130] I, along with many other pastors and lay leaders of mainline congregations, had become quite aware of some developing phenomena. Here is an overview of what we discovered:

- The preponderance of worshipers, as we mentioned earlier, came from among an older population, sixty or older, to be precise.
- Attendance in religious education programs for children had declined considerably.

---

129 This approach centered on an ongoing connection with the local church fostered by opportunities to share in worship structured by the pastor for their use at home. This was an important aspect of pandemic ministry in the church in which I was serving at the time. Thanks to a wonderful woman who helped coordinate this, we sent materials , including my message based on Scripture, to a number of people in our church who did not access worship online.

130 The pandemic began in March 2020, as noted previously.

- The number of people in mainline congregations participating in Confirmation programs had dropped.
- Large numbers of young adults, often with children, within local communities I served, had little to no connection with churches.
- Requests for baptizing children were declining in numbers.
- Active youth groups in these churches were falling into oblivion.
- Lay persons involved in church leadership, e.g. Church Council, tended to be older in years and it was becoming more and more difficult to enlist younger adults to participate. Side note: *Younger adults tended to be extremely busy for a lot of understandable reasons!*

For many of these faithful senior citizen churchgoers (By the way, at the time of this writing, that is what I have to call myself!), these trends were quite perplexing. Going to church on Sundays had long been part of their lives and they were bothered by the fact that those generations behind them did not share the same commitment. These wonderful, committed older churchgoers found themselves moved by nostalgia and yearning for the days when the church was filled with children and younger adults.

In my years as a pastor serving large numbers of older adults at a time when I was morphing into one myself, I found myself deeply impressed by their commitment to the church which they loved. I sympathized with their pain when they told me about churches they had attended for years that are now closing. No language referring to "Holy Closure" [131]would sooth them or take away their sense of loss or their pain.

Speaking of "Holy Closure".... With all due respect, I really DO NOT like the term. I will explain that in some detail below. However,

---

131 A term used for the culminating activity in the process of closing a local church. This is a term used within the Evangelical Lutheran Church in America. In the New England Synod of the ELCA, whose congregations I have served, there have been several instances of such " Holy Closure" over these past few years.

I believe it is important to explain what the term means and how a good number of people have been supportive of it:

WHAT IS HOLY CLOSURE?

To state it as directly as possible, the term "Holy Closure" is used within some churches as a formal process centered on the closing of a church. It culminates in a worship service which includes specific liturgical actions both celebrating the church's history and closing its doors. In addition, an integral part of this process is the church's sharing of its resources with some congregations that are remaining open. This is exemplified in many churches making significant contributions to both other churches and to many worthwhile causes.

A church in San Francisco offers us an excellent example as described in an article published by the ELCA: [132]

> *Grace Evangelical Council Treasurer Shelley Carroll began writing a list of all the items the church was looking to give to others: bookcases, cleaning supplies, a baptismal font, paraments, tables, a refrigerator, and so much more. As of last week, 15 congregations, mission partners or ecumenical organizations in our Synod had received gifts from Grace Evangelical to help further their ministry.*

AS I SEE IT...

In my opinion, this is clearly a good and a positive thing...

As we see from this example, there is a definite sense of outreach in this process of closure. It is clear that the act of closing also involves actions of giving which will help serve the ministry of other active churches. "Holy Closure" insures that a church will

---

132 This is found on the web site of the Sierra Pacific Synod: . Here is the link:
    https://www.spselca.net/post/when-one-church-door-closes-another-church-door-opens.

not simply close but instead that, in its closing, it will contribute to the ministry of other churches currently active.

In spite of the positives that are involved, to be perfectly honest, it is important that I make clear my concerns.

In doing so, I wish to provide you some excerpts from a recent post of the New England Synod, Evangelical Lutheran Church in America:[133]

"Amidst all that we are going through as church, we need to remember we are a death and resurrection faith," said Bishop James Hazelwood [134] *during a recent conversation at the Synod Council regarding the recently announced closings of six congregations in 2022.*

Last year several congregations voted to close their ministry, send members to nearby congregations and distribute assets to numerous ministries such as the ELCA World Hunger Appeal, Lutheran World Relief, Camp Calumet [135] and other likeminded church charitable organizations. These congregations have each held their last worship service. Some churches voted to merge with a nearby congregation.

In a recent report to the Synod Council, a consultant reported that she is now working with fourteen congregations who have asked for her guidance, as they explore merging with a nearby congregation, or concluding their ministry.

Here is what she said:

"As difficult as this is for our parishioners who are grieving the loss of their beloved congregations, it is also testimony to their generosity as they share their financial gifts with a variety of ministries - from local to global - and bring their God-given gifts to the mission at their new faith communities. A true resurrection story!"

Death is a prerequisite for new life. Pastor Josh Sullivan of the recently merged Christ the Good Shepherd, Hamden, CT reports

---

133 This was sent as part of an email to those on the Synod email list.

134 Bishop, New England Synod, ELCA.

135 An important ministry of the New England Synod, a place where our daughter spent time over the course of several summers in her youth. A wonderful place!

that one of the reasons their congregation is in the midst of rebirth is their willingness to die. *"It certainly doesn't come easy—facing any kind of death," Pastor Josh admits. "And I often will remind our folks that each predecessor church really did die. But I think in the moments when they accept that their old congregations have died, it really gives permission to let go of old habits and opens us to see together all the new things God is doing."*

"For the longest time we measured the success of the church with the ABCs – attendance, buildings and cash, " said Associate to the Bishop Rev. Sara Anderson, at a recent meeting of pastors who serve as deans. *"But it's clear the church as we knew it is dying. How will we redefine success not measured by those old standards? What does success look like when we trust in the resurrection?"* [136]

"I think this is a time of loss in the church. Many of us, myself included, grieve that decline of the church. " said Bishop Hazelwood. *"But, I've always maintained that God is birthing something new, and I still believe it. Though clearly we are in a time of loss right now, and that's particularly painful."*

When asked if there are any quick steps to fix the current decline of the church, the Bishop added, *"We live in an age of the quick fix. While that's what everyone wants, I'm not sure there is a quick fix to anything, ever. Instead of a fix, I'm an advocate of experimentation, exploring collaboration and living honestly into being the body of Christ. That means life, death and resurrection. We see life and resurrection in our churches, but often it requires Good Friday as a prerequisite to Easter."*

As Pastor Anderson has said, *"Our church was born in a tomb."*[137]

SOME OF MY THOUGHTS...

It is important that I place my response in context:

---

136 From a member of the staff of the ELCA, New England Synod.
137 Pastor Sara Anderson, Associate to the Bishop, also cited above. She certain makes a good point here....yes, it was!

Over these past few years, I, an ordained clergyperson in the United Church of Christ, have had the great opportunity to serve as a pastor in several Lutheran churches which are part of the New England Synod of the ELCA. As you know from reading this book, my movement away from Roman Catholicism and the ordained ministry within it was inspired by my fascination with Martin Luther and the Reformation dating back many years to my college days. Even when I wrote a paper explaining why I was seeking to enter the ministry of the United Church of Christ, I cited my deep regard for Martin Luther and his role in making possible the Reformation.

In addition, it was in churches within the ELCA and the wonderful pastors who served them that I was inspired to take steps that would eventually lead me to leave the Roman Catholic Church, something that WAS NOT an easy decision!

CHURCH CLOSURES

Over the last few years, I have witnessed firsthand the experience of church closures. In addition, I have also learned a lot about church mergers as well. As we know, a MERGER involves a sharing of resources between and among churches. With regard to specifics, in mergers, we will find clergypersons providing worship opportunities and other programs in more than one church. In my part of the country, along with others, in Catholic churches, this means a reduction in the number of Masses both on weekends and weekdays as well as the expectation that a presiding priest will travel to two or sometimes three congregations over the course of a weekend.

In the area in which I live, the most noteworthy examples of closures I have seen have taken place in the Episcopal Church and the Evangelical Lutheran Church in America. I am most familiar with the ELCA as I have served as a pastor in some of the churches of this denomination and have been actively involved in offering pulpit supply in those churches as well as serving a short term as an acting pastor while the church's pastor was on sabbatical leave. [138]

Since 2014, I have been most fortunate to have served churches in the ELCA even though I have been ordained in the United Church of Christ and retain my position as a clergyperson within that denomination. I was excited nearly 20 years ago when the ELCA was part of a group of many Protestant churches which came to a shared agreement within their denominations. This agreement made provisions for pastors ordained in some particular denominations to serve in others that were part of this agreement. In my case, I was interested in having the option to serve churches in the ELCA, where possible.[139]

As a result, in the several years prior to my retirement in 2021, I was privileged to serve as a pastor in two different ELCA churches in Central Connecticut and to provide three-month pastoral coverage for a Lutheran pastor while he was on sabbatical, as noted. When I retired, I was able to be placed on the Pulpit Supply list of both the ELCA and the UCC and have spent time leading worship and preaching within both denominations.

As an ordained clergyperson in the United Church of Christ in my part of the country, I have NOT witnessed a comparable number of closures. With some exceptions, many New England Congregational churches were established several centuries ago whereas the ELCA congregations, even those long established ones, came along much later. The first UCC church I served was founded in 1738, as an example! [140]

Conversely, many Lutheran churches established in my part of New England do NOT go back as far as do the churches in the

---

138 This is St. Paul's Lutheran Church in Wethersfield, Connecticut.
139 This is known as the Formula of Agreement.
140 UCC churches in New England, as a general rule, tend to go way back in time and are closely connected to the developing early history of the United States. The church to which I refer is the Congregational Church of Union, Connecticut, UCC , which I served from 2001 to 2012.

UCC. Many were established after World War 2, at a time when there was much growth and vitality in the institutional church.[141]

Over the course of the last several years, I have had firsthand knowledge through my readings and conversations with other pastors and with laypersons from various churches of several churches in the ELCA that are within a rather close distance to my home which have closed and have gone through this experience of Holy Closure. One was a church I had served as pastor for several years before it eventually shut down only a few years after I left.[142]

To reiterate what I mentioned above, I have also served as a pastor in congregations of the United Church of Christ as well, the church in which I was ordained and in which I remain a member. My experience in the UCC is that, while some closures have occurred and some churches are struggling with whether this is something with which they will need to deal rather soon, most of these churches in the geographical area in which I live have not closed and do not appear to be on the brink of doing so at this particular time.

I have also noticed an interesting phenomenon:

In some cases, the ELCA churches facing closure were established fairly late in the history of church planting in America. I am quite aware of ELCA churches closed in the early part of the 21st century that were not established until the late 1950's or sometime not long before. I would affirm that this fact is quite significant.

IS THIS REALLY WORTH BEING CONCERNED ABOUT?

One could legitimately say that to face this is simply to face reality and in this context, the ELCA has taken the right steps in the right direction.

YET…To be perfectly honest, this phenomenon concerns me. On the other hand, there is the very legitimate question here

---

141 This period is considered to be among the most active in the area of church development in the history of the United States.

142 This is Christ the King Lutheran Church in Windsor, Connecticut.

as to whether it should REALLY be a cause for concern! Let me explain…

QUITE THE JOURNEY…

In the interest of full disclosure, it is important that I give what I see as very important biographical background. Even if you have read my previous books where I allude to my movement out of the Catholic Church, you would not have read about this chain of events I describe below:

When I made the decision to consider leaving the Catholic Church, which I served as an ordained clergyperson, my first thought was to explore the possibility of becoming a pastor in the ELCA. There were two experiences that drove this reality, in addition to my honest self-reflection as to whether I could honestly remain in the Roman Catholic Church. *Looking back on my life, there was definitely a history to this:*

PLEASE READ THIS CAREFULLY…

When I was in college, I was inspired by a professor who happened to be Lutheran [143] and I also began attending the ELCA church at which he worshiped. [144] I was uplifted by the quality of both the worship and religious education programming offered there. I absolutely loved the Sunday morning forums as well as the weekly Sunday liturgies I attend. To put it mildly, I was really excited about Lutheranism because of the combination of ritual without extraneous activity within the ritual.

Many years later, I grew friendly with an ELCA pastor whom I had met through my wife's involvement in an ecumenical Bible Study. They were a wonderful couple and the pastor and I had become good friends, sharing an interest not only in matters religious but also things athletic as well. He and I attended basketball games

---

143 He was on the faculty of the Roman Catholic college which I attended.
       He is Dr. Dennis Ormseth.
144 Trinity Lutheran Church, Worcester, Massachusetts.

together [145] and when he and his family moved to Minnesota and were there at the time my daughter enrolled in a college in that state [146], he and I went to a college football game on Saturday night and a major league baseball game the next day in what was then the Metrodome in the city of Minneapolis. Years later, this pastor opted to leave the ELCA.

While I valued my ministry as a Catholic Permanent Deacon, as well as my work teaching religion classes and overseeing church youth groups and retreats, I was experiencing an internal struggle with the Roman Catholic Church. As a result of my background studying Luther in college, participating in worship in that wonderful Lutheran congregation and connecting with a person who was a Lutheran pastor who would go on to become my friend, I found myself facing a serious question, one getting more serious each and every passing day: *"Do I want to stay in the Catholic Church …or should I leave?"* [147]

By the time I had made the decision to start searching, the first place I went to was back to that Lutheran church. On the first morning I was there, I met the then relatively new pastor and I found him to be wonderful.[148] When my wife and I brought our children there, both Pastor Bill and the church's Associate Pastor[149] were fantastic! They were kind and extremely welcoming and were a GREAT pastoral team! I will ALWAYS be grateful for how they lived out their ministry.

As time moved along, I both made the decision to leave the Catholic Church as well as one to explore what I needed to do to become an ordained pastor in the ELCA.

To explore this, I reached out to the leaders of the New England Synod. I arranged for conversations with them and was very

---

145 UCONN basketball was and is quite popular where we live.

146 St. Olaf College, Northfield, Minnesota

147 The in depth details of this struggle can be found in my book *Crossing the Street, whose most recent second edition has been published by Energion Publications.*

148 Rev. Bill White.

149 Rev. Julie Reuning- Scherer.

grateful for the time they were willing to spend with me.[150] I made them aware of my past background and my academic background in college, graduate school and in the four-year formation program for Catholic men seeking to be ordained as Permanent Deacons. I explained to them in detail my ministry as a Catholic "Permanent Deacon."

Somewhere along the way, they suggested that I spend time at another Lutheran Church in Manchester under the supervision of its wonderful pastor.[151] *It was a great suggestion!* I really appreciated my conversations with her and the wonderful opportunities she gave me to preach and to lead discussions in the church. It was a great, albeit short lived experience. More about that is described below...

In addition, I attended an excellent conference at an ELCA church in Hartford [152] which focused on the newly developed Formula of Agreement [153] which opened possibilities for people ordained in one of the shared Protestant traditions to serve in a different one. I found the thinking behind this new formula to be wonderfully sensible and considerably groundbreaking.

Throughout this journey of mine, because of my ongoing conversation with leaders of the New England Synod, including with one who was assigned to help me through this process, what became clear was that my path to possible ordination in the ELCA was going to be difficult. The individual assigned to me in the Synod office was somewhat less than affirming.[154]

As I attempted to explain my academic background to him, with undergraduate and graduate degrees in the field of religious

---

150 Rev. Ted Asta.

151 Rev. Martha Klein Larson.

152 Emanuel Lutheran Church.

153 This statement offered information regarding the sharing of clergy to meet the needs of local churches from several mainline denominations.

154 I need to be clear that the way this person communicated with me did NOT reflect my overall interaction with the New England Synod. As noted above, Pastor Asta was outstanding, as were other ELCA clergy with whom I had conversations throughout this process!

studies and religious education, as well as a four year program of preparation for the ordained ministerial role of Permanent Deacon in the Catholic Church, along with my extensive work both teaching theology, Biblical studies and Christian ethics and working in a position of leadership on a Diocesan staff [155], it became clear to me that it may not be very easy at all for me to have the opportunity to serve in the ELCA in at least the near future.

Not long thereafter, in keeping with the innate kindness of the pastor at Emanuel, he took steps to coordinate a trip for the two of us down to the ELCA seminary he had attended in Philadelphia. The bottom line that became clear to me from my conversation with leadership of that seminary was that if I were to be considered for ordained ministry as a pastor in the ELCA, I would have needed to spend four years in Philadelphia at the Lutheran seminary there.

In terms of my ministry as a husband and a father, a rather significant lay ministry, I would say, I would NOT abandon my wife and growing children to spend time four hours away for five days a week and for most of the year. To be honest, it was my conviction that this seminary (and denomination) needed to deal better with certain individual situations, such as mine. [156]

Interestingly enough, as a result of the many changes occurring both in churches and seminaries, at the time of this writing in 2023, many denominations including the ELCA are offering a variety of options in their preparation of clergy. I can't say that such was the case at the time I describe above!

Honestly, I have known a good number of clergy of different denominations and Catholic priests as well who had very little undergraduate work done in areas of religion and theology. Many of them majored in a variety of different subjects. This is NOT a critical statement on my behalf as I am convinced that this knowl-

---

155 The Roman Catholic Diocese of Providence, where I was responsible for Youth Ministry from.1976-78.

156 As you can see, I have felt and still feel strongly about this!

edge can be most applicable in pastoral ministry.[157] In my case, I had both an undergraduate degree in Religious Studies, including immersion in Lutheran theology and thought through my course-work with the Lutheran pastor I mentioned previously. I also did graduate work under the tutelage of some distinguished theologians. In addition, I also feel that I had a good handle on the variety of trends in the church, both Roman Catholic and Protestant. *I am NOT saying that therefore the ELCA should have ordained me instantly, not at all. As a matter of fact, I was comfortable with the possibility of that not happening for 2 to 3 years!*

However, I remain convinced that during that time in the institutional church's life where things were really beginning to change on the seminary level, it was very important that church denominations open themselves to necessary adjustments in the overall process.

- I am pleased to say that I now see some positive movement in this direction. The increase in online educational options has helped in this regard, for sure![158]

THEREFORE:

Consequently, because of all of this, I decided that I could not take the steps at that time to travel to Philly and get the required training there to be ordained as a pastor in the ELCA. While I found that decision to be painful, it was really the only one that made any sense to me. I was NOT going to leave my family in Connecticut to spend most of my next few years in Philadelphia! If that meant no ordination, that was what was going to happen! While disappointed, I felt content with my process of decision making. *I wanted to be with my family!*

---

157 The institutional church benefits from those who have " real world" experience. Some of the finest pastors and priests whom I know had experience in other professions before they opted to pursue ordination.
158 A good number of seminaries across denominations are offering some online course options.

A NEW DIRECTION

To be honest, it did not take long for me to realize that I had made peace with my situation. I had a good job as a School Counselor and as a fervent baseball fan, I was fortunate to have opportunities to coach baseball on the high school and American Legion levels.[159] Those were important aspects of my life in those days and in doing them, along the way I was most fortunate to have spent considerable time coaching our two sons.[160] Much as Philly was a wonderful place, I would have missed the opportunity to drive both my sons and my daughter around to their many activities. Though one is busy from it, it is a great thing for a parent to experience the time spent with one's children!

HOWEVER:

Somewhere along the line, because of something I read on some web site, I discovered that a local congregation in the United Church of Christ had an opening for a person to direct Christian Education in that church. I applied, told them I was not a UCC member and when they asked what denomination or congregation I belonged to, I told them the truth and said *"Well, right now, I don't belong to one---and I am not really sure where I will end up"*.

They hired me for the job and I absolutely loved it! I had great regard for the two ministers who served there [161] and for the members of the congregation, including the person who chaired the search committee for a new DCE. [162] From a distance, I had great respect for the UCC but by working in a church of that de-

---

159 And we had some good teams!! All of this led to my eventually becoming the Head Baseball Coach at the school at which I worked. Just a few years later, a team I coached came very close to playing in the State Championship game. What added to the joy involved in this was that my youngest son was a member of the team!

160 Brian and Stephen LaRochelle, both of whom are educators and baseball coaches themselves!

161 Rev. Susan Prichard and Rev. Cynthia Carr.

162 The late Attorney Hal Cummings.

nomination and interacting regularly with two wonderful pastors, I came to learn so much more about it.[163]

Consequently, sometime along the way, I asked to meet with the UCC Committee on Ministry to discuss the possibilities of serving as a pastor in that denomination. The Committee interviewed me thoroughly and they ended up concluding that I had a good background in theology as well as a good ecumenical sense. They gave me the opportunity to be considered for ordained ministry in the not too distant future with the following provisions:

- I would be under the direction of a UCC pastor serving in my area of the state. I would have regular meetings with that pastor.
- I would maintain ongoing, regular contact with the Committee on Ministry of my Conference.
- I would work closely with the Committee on Ministry of the church I was serving and would need to get their endorsement.
- They also concluded that my academic background in religion, religious education and theology was solid BUT I would need to do specific work in the polity of the United Church of Christ [164] and take several credits in church related topics through distance learning options at a New England seminary with these courses required by and approved by the Committee on Ministry. In addition, I was required to attend an excellent program in New Hampshire which was centered on the process and polity that constituted possible ordained ministry in the UCC. It was a fantastic program! In my view, these recommendations made a great deal of sense and I embraced pursuing them! In fact, in retrospect, I have come to realize that the way the UCC structured opportunities for people to enter pastoral ministry offered a viable model for other denominations to follow.

---

163 As noted above.
164 This is something I looked forward to doing!

Over that period, I learned even more than I ever knew before about the breadth and depth of ecumenical Christianity.[165] I was eventually ordained in the UCC on March 2, 2002 at First Congregational Church, UCC, in Vernon. As the service ended, I walked down the aisle to the tune of *"A Mighty Fortress is Our God",* [166] processing out alongside one of the pastors from Emanuel Lutheran who was there when I was part of that congregation and was so helpful and kind to me. [167]

I proceeded to serve as pastor in congregations within the UCC and I loved it.[168] In 2014, Pastor Bill White asked me if I would be interested in serving with him at a Lutheran church in Windsor, Connecticut. *How about life coming full circle?* This was the man who was so good to me, even to the point of taking me to Philadelphia and reaching out to others on my behalf. I will always be grateful!

His suggestion was approved by those in charge on the Synod level [169]and both the Bishop and the pastor assigned to oversee the region in which the church resided came to meet with me and with Pastor Bill. [170]

---

165 As much as I thought I knew about ecumenism, I discovered I had even more to learn!

166 My favorite hymn, written by Martin Luther!

167 Pastor Julie!

168 I first served at the Congregational Church of Union, Connecticut from 2001-2012. This church was really kind to me, including offering financial support to me when I went to Chicago to earn my doctorate through the D. Min in preaching program. From 2012-14, I served as a pastor at Second Congregational Church in Manchester, UCC,

169 Bishop James Hazelwood and Rev. Paul Sinnott who was a fantastic resource for me through my years serving ELCA churches. Side note: Bishop Hazelwood has written some excellent books that are well worth reading! I also commend his online writings which are available on the Internet.

170 Throughout my time serving ELCA churches, I was most grateful for Rev. Sinnott's insight and support! We had the opportunity to communicate frequently and I deeply appreciated that!

When Pastor Bill left this congregation, I remained as their pastor. When I decided eventually to leave that church in 2017 as I was quite busy in my counseling job at the school where I still worked, I remained quite active as someone on the supply list of pastors who were approved by the Synod and the UCC Committee on Ministry[171] to serve in both ELCA and UCC churches. In 2019, I was offered the position of pastor at Grace Lutheran, ELCA, in Plainville, Connecticut, where I served until October of 2021. Since then, I have remained active as a UCC pastor doing supply worship leadership in both denominations. In the past year, in fact, I have offered workshops centered on topics covered in my books at the gatherings of both the UCC and the ELCA in the New England area.

What a ride it has been.....a ride for which I am most grateful!

I am deeply thankful for the opportunities I have had to serve as a pastor within the Evangelical Lutheran Church in America. When I began pondering quite seriously the possibility of leaving Roman Catholicism when I was serving within it as a Permanent Deacon, as you know from reading this, the very first congregation I visited to help me process a possible move into Protestantism was a Lutheran church. As I have noted, when I was in college and exploring the world of ecumenism within Christianity, a church I spent a lot of time in was a wonderful Lutheran church in Worcester, Massachusetts. As a student at a Jesuit Catholic college [172], one of my most highly respected professors was a Lutheran pastor and I am most grateful for having had the opportunity to share many discussions with him regarding the Reformation and Lutheranism in particular.

Were one to look at the religious expression known as Lutheranism, one would find a rather incredible history. What we now call Lutheran reflects a church denomination that changed the course of religious history. I am talking here about the Reformation, of course! One could make a case that, even without Luther, there

---

171 The committee that oversees such matters.
172 Holy Cross.

would have been breakaways from the Catholic Church. However, most scholars would acknowledge, I think, that if one is looking for the real trigger to the Reformation, one must look at Martin Luther and how he shaped the church.

The interesting thing is that even though Lutheranism DID represent a breakaway from the dominant Roman Catholicism of its day, it retained much of Catholicism's worship practice. Of course, depending on geographical location, the worship practices within Lutheranism were different from place to place, yet much of the CORE of Lutheran worship was based on a REFORMED version of Roman Catholic liturgy as well as theology.

In addition, Lutheranism has long had its heroes, so to speak, with Martin Luther and Katie Von Bora [173] being noteworthy examples. However, Lutheranism scrapped the concept of the intercession of the saints and indulgences that would cut one's time in Purgatory short, and espoused a theology that, while similar in many ways to that found in Martin Luther's lived Catholicism, was significantly different and signaled an important break from Rome and some of its doctrines and dogmas. Much of the core of the Lutheran approach both in its nascent days and throughout history can be found in Luther's *Small Catechism.* [174]

Even though I decided not to pursue ordination in the ELCA, my respect for Lutheran Christianity has never waned and I was most grateful for the Formula of Agreement[175] which made possible my service as a pastor for many years within Lutheran churches as well as someone who could lead worship in them in my capacity as an approved " supply pastor".[176]

---

173 His wife!

174 I highly recommend that you read it, both carefully and often!

175 As described earlier.

176 A pastor who is available to lead worship and preach when clergy from that congregation are not available. Since I retired in 2021, I have been doing a great deal of supply preaching in many different congregations, as well as some different denominations.

My Concern:

To cut to the chase, my concern centers on this:

In the closures of so many ELCA churches as well as the struggles to be found within Lutheranism in general, I worry that a very important part of church history as well as liturgical practice is falling by the wayside.

When I think of Protestantism and its history, with due respect to all of the important figures in that history, I see Martin Luther as a driving force and the expression of Christianity found in the churches that in some way bear his name (though he would have hated that)[177] to be important to keep alive as part of the overall American religious scene. PERHAPS I AM NOT SEEING THE BIG PICTURE...

WHAT DO YOU THINK? I am serious - I really would love to know your opinion. [178] Even with my concern, I must acknowledge the possibility that I am missing something! Quite honestly, as you read this book, I would be curious as to how you view what I have said about the church closure issue.

For example, in my native New England, I am witnessing incredible work centered on collaboration among different mainline denominations. To the credit of ELCA leadership in New England [179], SIGNIFICANT work has been done bringing together Lutheran and Episcopal congregations, as well as sharing in worship and educational programming with churches of the long-standing United Church of Christ in New England. While these churches may have some liturgical differences and points of theological difference, they, at core, share the essentials of a common faith.

Since I have been so concerned about the decline found within the Episcopal Church and the emergence of all kinds of "breakaway" Anglican churches that oppose women's ordination and which have an aversion to openness to those of varied sexual

---

177 He thought it was Jesus' church, not his!!
178 Please feel free to post on the Facebook page that goes by the title of this book or the page with my name on it!
179 Under the leadership of Bishop Hazelwood!

orientations and that have joined hands with conservative Catholics and Protestant evangelicals, I am heartened in seeing the activities and opportunities found within the Episcopal churches in my native New England AND the role of ELCA leadership in this region in forging some truly outstanding ecumenical ventures, including those with the Episcopal Church and the United Church of Christ!

While at the time of this writing, there are significant tensions occurring within the national setting of the ELCA[180], I am grateful for the leadership of those in the local Lutheran Synod who have worked so hard and been so kind to me in giving me wonderful opportunities to serve as well! -

Over the years, dating back to my high school days in Connecticut, I have had great respect for and interest in the history and theology found within different mainline denominations. I have discovered points of connection between and among them that are important while, at the same time, valuing those aspects of church polity and liturgical practice that are somewhat distinctive from one another while still expressive of a shared unity.

I am most impressed with the hard work that has been put into resource materials to help assist clergy and congregations in developing a variety of liturgical styles. However, I have also learned from experience that within congregations in many denominations one will find a reluctance to embrace some of the changes necessary to implement those worship experiences. From my experience leading worship in many different congregations and some different denominations, I have discovered that some churches continue to be years behind much of the liturgical renewal found within their denominations and mainline Christianity as well.

I have visited churches in several Protestant denominations whose worship style and material has not changed much over the

---

180 Several articles are accessible online to fill in some of the details as well as on the "EXPOSING THE ELCA" blog! This blog is run by those who have broken away from the ELCA. I find their posts consistently troubling!

years and does not reflect some of the options available in the worship resources of their denominations.

Two of the finest available resources that I have found are the WORSHIP WAYS material published by the UCC and the SUNDAYS AND SEASONS material from the Evangelical Lutheran Church in America.[181] I know that there are others as well. My familiarity with these comes from the experience of serving congregations in both of those denominations.

My suggestion is that congregations would draw on the resources available from within their denomination and work on implementing what they find within them! In addition, I also suggest that worship leaders explore the broad range of materials available from a number of outstanding online resources.

While not as conversant in what is accessible in the resources offered in some other Protestant mainline churches, I have discovered helpful materials in those as well. I have integrated many of them into worship I have led in both ELCA and UCC congregations.

A TROUBLING REALITY ...

I was quite troubled recently when I was invited to preach at a UCC church in the town whose ELCA congregation I had most recently served. As I walked out of the church building that morning after worship, I could not help but notice that perpendicular to where I was stood a building that once housed an Episcopal Church, the church whose closure was troubling to so many of its members, including those who would eventually become members of the local Lutheran Church in that town where I had served as pastor.[182] That Episcopal church was now closed. That same morning, in the UCC church, a woman introduced herself who told me that she used to be a member of that Episcopal church across the street. She mentioned that while some others chose to

---

181 Excellent resources!
182 Plainville, Connecticut.

join the ELCA church in town, she opted to belong to this UCC congregation. [183]

This visceral reaction of mine that I really WISH this Episcopal church had NOT closed comes from a place within my heart which holds to a strong belief in the value found in historic mainline Protestantism, an approach to Christianity which offers great possibilities for ecumenical connections. This tendency to seek a sense of unity is reflected in the establishment of such organizations as the World Council of Churches and the National Council of Churches as well. In addition, one finds it in the commitment to the Week of Christian Unity that has been part of Protestant Christianity in the United States for many years. Unfortunately, as the years have rolled along, the celebration of this week with shared worship being an important part of the experience, has been fading away gradually.

HOWEVER:

During the time that I have served as pastor in several mainline Protestant churches, many of the congregants within those churches, including those in my most recent pastorate, made mention to me of how they wished that "our church" could do some of the things that these other churches in town were doing. They were referring here to conservative, evangelical churches of varied denominations as well as to newly planted independent congregations.

To them, the idea of going to church for worship was integral to their lives and they found themselves wondering why if these conservative churches could draw young people and families, then why couldn't ours? While this provided me the opportunities to teach about differences and distinctions in theology among churches, including the dangers in so called "evangelical Christianity in America" [184] and even to present information to these wonderful

---

183 The Congregational Church of Plainville, UCC.
184 A real concern of mine is that many people do not understand the major differences between mainline and conservative Christianity. As I see it,

people about the history of religion, this was most certainly not easy and here is why:

For great numbers of adults in mainline congregations, mean-ingful adult education has not been a priority within their church communities. A knowledge of historical background and a developed sense of both Scripture and the history of the institutional church are very much lacking. The result of this is that it leads to an inability to discern the differences within expressions of Christianity.

Please understand that while this seems critical, it is not in-tended to be an attack on anyone's faith!

In the years since I began serving in Protestant congregations, I have noticed a distinctive slippage in the offering of programs in adult education. I see that decline as I peruse the bulletins and web sites of many Protestant congregations as well. I look for these things and get excited when I see them and quite saddened when I don't! On the other hand, I am thrilled when, at some churches where I have gone to do pulpit supply, the church bulletin included information about discussions and book studies that were being offered in that church. What a wonderful thing! [185]

Many of the dedicated people whom I have known within congregations I have served have offered some sincere suggestions to help increase attendance at worship as well as to engage more young people and their parents. Well intentioned individuals have come up with ideas such as posting flyers on the bulletin boards of local supermarkets and other places of business, handing out church pens and mugs, inviting adults to worship and advertising opportunities for young people to attend Movie Nights or to be part of a Youth Group. Much of this communication to youth is directed toward people who have not had a church connection for quite a while or who never have had one in the first place.

---

this is an outgrowth of inadequate religious educational programming within a great number of churches.

185 Examples include: Orange Congregational Church, Second Congregational, Stafford UCC, First Baptist, Meriden (American Baptist).and St. Matthew's Lutheran Church in Avon, Connecticut.

Many of these youth are quite busy as, in addition to their schoolwork, they have jobs and work several hours each week and are involved in all kinds of activities such as sports, dance and clubs to which they belong in school and which they really enjoy. They would most likely see the invitation to add a church activity to this as not being of much interest as they are already not connected to the church, nor do they tend to have many friends who are. Why add one more thing to an already busy schedule?

SO HERE ARE SOME SUGGESTIONS...

- First and foremost, a congregation needs to find ways to get past the nostalgic mentality which I would call *"the way we were"*. Conversations and presentations within the congregation need to focus on the simple reality that times have changed. While easier said than done, it ABSOLUTELY must happen!!
- While that may sound threatening to many, the reality of history is that times have changed many, many times. The examples are considerable. They are reflected in churches, often subtly, but reflected nonetheless.
- Secondly, it is important to reexamine the structures within the congregation. While each local church has its own structures and traditions, it is also obvious that the ways in which church participation is structured has a certain commonality to it which spans several generations and may not be as effective now as it used to be back then!

While there is a certain level of comfort in churches embracing some of their traditions, they also need to remain open to the possibility that some, NOT ALL, of those traditions are particularly relevant right now to the church in its current setting. While churches within different denominations have different language to describe leadership roles within their community, most churches include the roles I list below as part of their organizational structure. These include:

- An elected Church Council with term limits
- A church treasurer
- Subcommittees led by individual members of the Church Council
- A Council President who is seen as the "lay leader" of the congregation

One can make a case that organizational structure is needed and that these are important roles. However, the reality is that people within the congregation who are NOT in these positions could see those who are as having a greater responsibility for the management of the church than does the average "person in the pew". This, of course, could become a problem BUT not as great a problem as the fact that this approach, top heavy as it is, does not provide room for greater participation by many in the overall leadership of the church.

THE PROCESS OF REEXAMINATION WITHIN THE LOCAL CHURCH

In my view, the STARTING POINT for a church's self-examination is twofold:

1. This consists of serious congregation wide conversation about that which the church really needs, a process facilitated by the Church Council.
2. It also emphasizes the empowerment of those interested in helping to make those needs possible.

HOW MIGHT THIS WORK?

I believe that this process all starts with two basic questions that should be asked within the entire congregation AND WITH ITS GUESTS!

1. *What would you like to see happen within this church?*

2. *Is what you would like to see DOABLE at this time? DOABILITY IS ABSOLUTELY CRUCIAL... Many great ideas have failed in many organizations, the church included, when ideas perceived as exciting and great have simply NOT passed the DOABILITY TEST.[186]*

This would all lead to two more things to consider:

3. *How willing would you be to help coordinate this effort within the congregation AND to explore ways that this might also be of interest to people not currently connected with this congregation?*
4. *Even more important would be the level of energy you realistically believe you could bring to this task! The number of uncompleted projects found within organizations such as the church and others is quite astonishing! I tend to dub this the "Wouldn't it be nice if?" syndrome!*

Dealing with some Possible Impediments:

THIS IS HUGE- WHY BE PART OF A WASTE OF TIME??

A member of a church leadership team, e.g. a Church Council member, most likely has a busy life. She or He might very well have work, family, and other volunteer commitments in addition to being expected to participate in a regularly scheduled Council meeting.

Side Note:

It is REALLY important that the church has at least one representative from its youth as part of the Council AND that the opinions of those representatives are RESPECTED by the adults in the room!

---

186 Simply put, this involves asking the question to be found in every ideal, i.e. IS THIS DOABLE HERE AND NOW.....IN OUR TIME AND PLACE?

HOWEVER:

It is possible that the idea you have might lead to an increase in energy and commitment both from people within the congregation AND from those not connected with this church but who would find a particular "outside of the box" activity to be quite intriguing.

It is ALSO POSSIBLE that your idea is one which really motivates you and that you would be downright excited about putting your heart and soul into it.

Let's explore a HYPOTHETICAL example, one based on real life possibilities:

Person A is an elected member of the Church Council. She is very comfortable participating in monthly Council meetings and giving her opinions about what is and what should be going on in the life of her congregation. However, when asked to consider what her church really needs and what she would like to see happen within it, she has some ideas and some questions that have not been part of the Council's regular agenda.

WOULDN'T IT BE NICE IF?

- *Ideally, what would be wonderful is if each member of a Church Council were to see herself/himself as expected to offer suggestions for church related activities and encouraged as well to be free to "play to their strengths", i.e. to communicate and coordinate possible activities within the congregation and the local community which flow from those things about which they are quite passionate.*

- What I have learned over the years is that most people committed to various organizations have within themselves an imbedded sense best articulated as a "Wouldn't it be nice if?" mentality.

HOWEVER...

The "wouldn't it be nice if approach" also has its limitations. I have discovered in various settings in which I have worked, including those outside of the church, that it simply is not enough to toss out new ideas. Included in their presentation needs to be specific plans for their actual implementation. In fact, ideas WITHOUT a plan for implementation can lead to eventual significant frustration! It would be interesting to see how many ideas that have been floated within congregations never came to fruition! To be honest, this has been one of the most noticeable issues I have seen in many organizations, churches NOT excluded!

NOT NOSTALGIA

Churches that have been around for a while tend to have some traditions which members and friends of the church see as important in the life of their communities. In churches that I have served, I have experienced the importance of some of these traditions. They have ranged from special programs the church has offered to special events such as annual tag sales and other activities in which church members have been involved and members of local communities have enjoyed attending. In churches where I have worked, these have included all kinds of special annual events to which long standing members of the congregation have really looked forward to hosting and implementing. I have found over the years that people work extraordinarily hard to make these events worthwhile.[187]

- It is not my intention to dismiss the value or importance of these events in the life of the local church. What I would like to suggest, however, is that churches take special care to broaden the range of possible activities that their own members and friends as well as those locals not connected to the church see as of value.

187 I am thinking of such events as tag sales, bake sales, church dinners and many more, all dependent upon the congregation's background and history.

• My underlying premise is that while events that have been part of church life for a while may very well still be relevant, that relevance has to be explored. In that exploration, churches need to be sure to open themselves up to the possibilities of new events that may bring along with them a unique relevance and might attract people of different generations.

• I would also suggest (and this is important!) that while church leaders, such as Council members, should play a significant role in organizing and planning these events, the church needs to look at how what they do can appeal to a broader base than it has in the past.

In other words, church leaders should be actively engaged in seeking to recruit others. It should not always be "the same people." I say this recognizing the challenge involved in recruiting new people. Nevertheless, in the big picture and the "long run", I think it is worthwhile!

• In addition, volunteering to oversee a relatively short term event or project is far more palatable to many people than having a commitment of twelve months in length. In fact, the shorter-term leadership commitment really plays to the strengths of the one doing the committing and could very well be a most valuable asset for the church.

• Who knows? Those new recruits may end up being in charge one day! Of course, this COULD be bothersome to others who see their participation as part of the core group implementing an event as a major contribution they make to the church.

They are right! It is - BUT opening up to new, active participants can both provide a stronger structure for the future AND safeguard against the reality of BURNOUT.[188]

• There is much joy to be found in an outdoor tag sale come Spring or Fall which takes place in the parking lot or front

---

188 Burnout can be a huge impediment in church life!

lawn of the church. What is especially joyful is when a good number of people from the community and surrounding communities come and spend some money! There is also a healthy camaraderie that can take place among those of different ages who are connected to the church, including its younger members so long as they are valued and treated respectfully.[189]

• However, the events that are part of a church's life SHOULD NOT BE LIMITED to "those things we have always done" alone. Those church traditions should always be reexamined with a hope that they may still be worth the time and energy [190] yet with a recognition that if they are not, it is perfectly OK to move on to other projects and ideas which will engage people of varied ages who are either part of that church or of the broader community. So, YES - It is possible that a church can survive well EVEN if one of its annual events does not take place, in which case an effort to institute a successful NEW event might very well make a real difference!

• Consequently, what is REALLY IMPORTANT is for churches to engage in discussing a wider range of possibilities for church activity. Let's examine this by using an example that while not reflecting specifics of a particular church is one to which many people connected to churches can relate:

THE PURPOSE OF CHURCH EVENTS

Events that churches sponsor tend to have two primary objectives:

---

189 Oftentimes, youth are treated poorly. They are often seen as people who can help do some necessary work and not as those who have insights on church life they could share!

190 I have seen people who have worked hard in church events express feelings of being absolutely "burned out" and annoyed by the fact that most other church members and friends have not helped out!

1. *They can create an atmosphere wherein people in the church are connecting with one another by working together.*
2. *They can bring in in some money to support the work of the church.*

That sounds simple, doesn't it? And it is also real!!

BROADENING THE POSSIBILITIES

What I want to suggest is that churches examine the possibilities for what they offer to insure that a broad range of people associated with the church are comfortable with being engaged in these activities AND so that others are comfortable with making suggestions for activities that have never been thought of within that particular congregation before.

Throughout the years I have served as a pastor in different congregations, I have seen this engagement of both regular church leaders, of volunteers and of the young people who are part of the church work out in various positive ways.

Here are a few examples:

*   When I served as a pastor at a small rural church in Connecticut's smallest town, we invited Bryan Nurnberger of the organization SIMPLY SMILES to come and speak at worship.[191] Something quite amazing happened as a result. First of all, the congregation was inspired to donate a considerable amount of money to this wonderful organization. Secondly, the young people in the congregation went out of their way to raise money as well. What was most fascinating was the passion our youth had for the prospect of possibly going out to the reservation in South Dakota and serving the children there who were helped through Simply Smiles.
*   While our youth were too young to do so at the time, their enthusiasm was amazing as was their feeling for the importance

---

191 I highly recommend that you go to simplysmiles.org to read about this amazing organization.

of serving others, something that they did in many ways in that church throughout their adolescent years. I remember with fondness all of their enthusiasm for finding ways to support those in need. They would stand out on the street both freely and enthusiastically and invite people driving by to stop and discuss the ways in which they could be of help as they took their considerable donations, all on the street of Connecticut's smallest town.[192]

• In addition, one night at that same little church,[193] we brought in some local youth with a background in music to offer a program to members of the congregation and the wider community. The free will offering which was received was quite significant. People enjoyed the event and a worthwhile local cause benefited as well!

• A few years later at another church, Christ the King ELCA in Windsor, Connecticut [194], with the help and support of the young people there, we organized a concert to support the victims of the Flint Water Crisis. This was a major concern at the time and remains one even years later. In addition, we brought in the renowned singer/song writer Kristen Graves[195] to do a couple of concerts, with none of the money going to the church but rather to some causes supported by our youth. When I served a church in Manchester, Connecticut, [196] where there was considerable poverty and hunger, once again, we were able to organize a concert where not one penny would go to the church. In one relatively brief evening event, we raised over $1200 for an organization that served the poor and the homeless of that community at a time when homelessness was on the rise!!

---

192 Union, Connecticut, population at the time around 600.
193 The Congregational Church of Union, UCC.
194 A church that went through " Holy Closure" in 2022.
195 An amazing musician!
196 Second Congregational Church, UCC.

- When I served my most recent church[197], we made plans for a concert where the proceeds would go completely to the needs of those in poverty. Despite some initial pushback because the proceeds would not go to the church itself, the congregation supported it and was all set to be quite engaged in this event. Sadly, it never happened because COVID-19 hit.[198]
- As I have mentioned earlier, in the most recent church in which I had served, we organized an ecumenical Youth Night where part of the program would be to see how we could bring young people together to meet the needs of others within the communities we served. This would have included youth not only from our church but also from churches within a radius of several miles!

BROADENING ONE'S AWARENESS

In making these suggestions, what I am advocating for is two-fold:

- Opportunities for broader engagement among members and friends of the church, young and old
- A willingness to think outside of the box both in terms of how people participate in the church and in the ways they plan for what the church provides the broader community

BACK TO WHERE WE BEGAN: THE WORDS OF BOB DYLAN

Please don't see this as being redundant. There is a reason why I am ending this chapter with the same words with which it began, these words of Bob Dylan:

Come gather 'round people wherever you roam
And admit that the waters around you have grown

197 Grace Lutheran Church in Plainville, Connecticut.
198 See details earlier in this book.

And accept it that soon you'll be drenched to the bone
If your time to you is worth saving
Then you better start swimming or you'll sink like a stone
For the times, they are a-changin'.[199]

There is no way that Bob Dylan had the institutional church in mind when he wrote the lyrics with which we began this chapter. To say otherwise would be a ridiculous stretch! As you now finish reading it, I would suspect that you may have a question or two as to why I cited a quote from one of his most well-known songs. You may wonder about how they would have any applicability to the functioning of this institution we call the church.

THEREFORE …

Let's take a few minutes to break down some of his best-known words:

- ADMIT THAT THE WATERS AROUND YOU HAVE GROWN

  It is important for churches to realize that things are different now. Churches no longer function the way that they used to do! Simply put: It is now a different world out there… This world of the church! Churches are immersed in something akin to deep water, for sure!

- ACCEPT IT THAT SOON YOU'LL BE DRENCHED TO THE BONE

  The result for many mainline churches is the possibility of closure. That has become an obvious reality!!

- THEN YOU BETTER START SWIMMING OR YOU"LL SINK LIKE A STONE.

---

199 Bob Dylan.

This swimming might very well entail new ideas and new directions! Churches may find that the way things have been done just won't work anymore but also discover that this is quite OK…

To avoid this scenario, churches have to think outside of the box.

- FOR THE TIMES THEY ARE A CHANGIN'

Acceptance of this can be difficult, but necessary!

That's enough Dylan for now [200] — but PLEASE give these words some thought!

---

200 Can one ever have enough Dylan?

5

MAKING PEACE WITH CLOSURE: GOOD OR BAD?

I have a confession to make....

As I noted in the last chapter, the fact that so many "mainline" Christian churches have closed over these last few years AND the projections that many more will do so in the not too distant future really bothers me. In this chapter, I would like to delve into this fact a little more deeply! What exacerbates me even more is that in many communities with which I am quite familiar, there are a variety of Christian churches outside of the well-known historic ones that are very active and thriving.

To be clear, my problem is NOT the fact that there is a variety of churches out there. It IS with the troubling fact that within Protestantism the so called "mainline" churches have dropped in attendance or have simply closed. You might ask what my issue would be with that. Some might say that so long as one is "going to church", what difference does it make if one is attending an ELCA, UCC, Presbyterian, Episcopal, Disciples of Christ, some other mainline church OR one of the more contemporary churches, often quite independent even when linked to a broader denomination?

As examples which are based on my own geographic area in New England, within a radius of approximately twenty miles, one of the two Episcopal churches in our town closed just a few months after we moved in. I am assuming there is no connection there! In addition, the ELCA church I served for four years as a pastor closed just a few months before I started writing this book, as well as a Lutheran church right over the line is nearby Western Massachusetts and one close in the Greater Hartford area. Within the New England Synod several closures have occurred over the last few years, including some in my home state of Connecticut and those members of a good number of congregations which remain open also express serious concern about the possibility that they may be shut down in the not so distant future.

As you know from reading about my background, I was raised Roman Catholic. When I attended college in Worcester, Mass and was in the process of exploring the possibility of the priesthood in the Roman Catholic Church, I was also drawn as I have mentioned in this book to the theological writings of Martin Luther and engaged in the process of exploring both one of the Lutheran congregations in Worcester, as well as other mainline Christian churches.[201]

In retrospect, I can see the naivete I possessed as a nineteen and twenty-year old. I was excited about exploring both the theology and the liturgical practices within Lutheranism. What I discovered in doing so was something I have found in other Protestant denominations as well:

I learned that many, maybe most, people who were Lutheran or Episcopal or any other Protestant mainline denomination for that matter AND most people who, like me, were Roman Catholics, landed in their churches and denominations NOT necessarily because they had a particular affinity for the theology and liturgical practices of that church, but rather because that was the worship tradition in which they were raised.

The reality for many of them was that they could identify things about other religious traditions with which to be critical while, at the same time, not necessarily sensing the presence of definite commonalities between and among varied expressions of Christian faith. This, in my view, was the result of a religious ed-

201 Trinity Lutheran Church, Worcester, Massachusetts.

ucation based on an INTERNAL view, i.e. the view held by and established in the doctrines of the particular religious tradition and denomination in which they were raised. It certainly was the view in which I was immersed as a Catholic! Please understand that I am stating this factually and not critically. Simply put, it is what it is and we are ALL shaped in our thinking and affiliations with that which we have been taught in many different ways throughout our lives.

As we know, because of societal changes which have impacted churches, the probability was that subsequent generations of ELCA Lutherans, Episcopalians, other mainline Protestants, as well as Roman Catholics, did not have the commitment to the practices of those traditions that people of previous generations in their families had. In fact, to be honest, much of the connection to a church or denomination would most likely NOT be based on the theological nuances of each established church. As a former teacher, occasionally, when offering presentations on the relationship between Protestantism and Catholicism in churches, I would have people respond to a questionnaire about the similarities and differences to be found in various Christian churches. I can't say that the scores were terribly high!

In essence, one went to a church because one was raised in a tradition or married into it. I quickly discovered that, while not alone, I was something of an exception. I was exploring Protestantism NOT because I was a Catholic frustrated by many of the rules of my church but rather because I was interested in the THEOLOGY of the Reformation, as expressed through the teachings, writings and example of Martin Luther.

I am convinced that this is a very IMPORTANT distinction! I had enough of a sense that my Catholicism's comfort level with issues of CONSCIENCE helped me see the inherent in depth value of Catholicism itself. AND… I remain, to this day, someone very proud of my Catholic heritage, flawed that it may be [202], and

---

202 To be clear, Protestantism is flawed as well!

deeply indebted to much of Catholic theological thinking as well as many facets of liturgical practice.

THERE IS ANOTHER REASON ...

There is another reason why some move away from the church in which they were raised. This is most noticeable within Roman Catholicism where it has to do with the topic of divorce and remarriage. As one who used to work with Catholics seeking annulments, I can attest to the difficulties inherent in the process, many of which end up keeping people away from pursuing them. Unfortunately, many people find that this process has led to them being estranged from the Catholic Church. Some actively seek engagement in a Protestant denomination while others simply remove themselves from participation in Catholic worship.

WHY AM I BRINGING THIS ALL UP?

This is a good question, right? In fact, I raise these issues as part of a chapter which I have labeled as *"Making Peace with Closure."* To be clear, while I DO accept the fact that sometimes churches must close, I have an issue with being comfortable about closing a church. I am aware that some churches are able NOT to close because they have good long-term financial endowments. I also understand that many congregations in some denominations [203] only got started during the prime of church growth, i.e. the late 1950S or early 1960's.

As a former pastor of one church which was established in 1738 [204] and another in 1889 [205], I understand that with long term financial commitments, older churches have more money to draw on than churches that evolved just a few decades ago. In addition, they may have many long-time members whose families date way back in the life of that church. Those individuals may be very likely

---

203 An example in my native New England is the ELCA.
204 Congregational Church of Union, CT, UCC.
205 Second Congregational Church, Manchester, CT, UCC.

to include leaving money to the church as part of their wills. This can make for financial benefits in a church's life!

I am also cognizant of the fact that those churches which do not have many ethnic groups in their area that relate to certain denominations would have a struggle to establish and build a church. These facts, when placed alongside the realities of diminished church attendance, make the possibility of church closure a reality that hovers over many a church. In addition, however, and I find this troubling, many of these churches tend not to go out of their way to reach out to those in their area who come from different backgrounds. This is quite unfortunate!

SOMETHING TO CONSIDER

This past year, as I noted previously, a church that I had served as a pastor from 2014-2017 closed. This church, an ELCA congregation, was in an active suburb of Hartford. This suburb is a well-integrated town with churches from a wide variety of religious traditions housed there. This Lutheran church was established in the late 1950's which was a long time after the founding of the UCC church in that community, one of the first established in Connecticut in the 1700's.[206] There was also a long-standing Catholic presence there with two established Roman Catholic churches in town.

- *As noted above, I left this church in 2017 as I was still finishing up my career as a full time School Counselor and opted to be available to do pulpit supply rather than continue working as many hours as I was in trying to keep up with the requirements of being a pastor. After I left, the church was served by a well experienced interim pastor, as well as two other pastors who were ordained in the ELCA, both of whom had excellent backgrounds.*
- *While since 2017, I have been removed from the workings of this church as all pastors should be once they leave a congregation, I*

---

206 Windsor, Connecticut. There is unending dispute…Oldest town in CT or is it Wethersfield?

must be honest and say that I was saddened by the closure of this church.

In addition, a few years after I left my position as pastor there, I officiated at the funeral of a former member of that church which was held in a Lutheran church in Massachusetts, in the town where he and his wife lived. They had joined this hometown church after the congregation in Connecticut shut down. As they had no pastor on board at the time of the man's death, I was asked to do the funeral. Soon thereafter I discovered that this church was in the process of considering what ELCA congregations call *"Holy Closure."*[207] Several months later, that church officially closed.

• A few years back, yet another ELCA church in the town of Ellington, Connecticut, a few miles away from where my wife and I live closed as well. I also understand that they ended up merging with an ELCA church several miles down the road, which is a positive thing.

In addition, just a few weeks before I was writing this page, two other ELCA churches in a Hartford suburb also shut down.[208] This has also been the case in many churches of which I have been aware both in my home state of Connecticut and over the line in Massachusetts.

HONEST SELF REFLECTION

I would be lying to you if I did not say how much the closures of churches bothers me. *I say this even while affirming that in some cases IT IS NECESSARY!* From what I am seeing in the statistics and what I am feeling experientially, this is happening quite a bit in a church that I have served, the Evangelical Lutheran Church in America, ELCA. *I must confess that I have some strong feelings about this yet, at the same time, I recognize that I am not either a member*

---

207 See previous chapter.
208 In Kensington and East Hartford, Connecticut.

nor a pastor at any of these closed churches and do not have all the background or details.

Nonetheless, I REALLY LIKE THE ELCA and am so grateful that I have been given opportunities to serve within it. In addition, as I stated earlier, I have a lot of respect for the leaders I have known who serve in the New England Synod. Consequently, these words of mine are NOT intended as an attack on anyone. *I cannot say that strongly enough!* However, I think it is fair for me to express what concerns me about this.

I ask that you read my comments carefully and as you process them, I encourage you to feel free to respond to me, either in a review of this book that you may write, a critique of it in some publication or by giving me your opinion through your correspondence with me.

A Brief Overview

- As I write this expression of concern for what has been happening in a particular church denomination, I do so aware that, at the same time, major issues are occurring in other mainline churches with which I am most familiar. I have witnessed the closing of some Episcopal churches throughout different areas in my native Connecticut, including the one I had enjoyed attending back when I was living in my home town of Putnam and had already embarked upon my youthful "religious search."

- Statistics indicate that Methodist churches have also gone into a split and a decline [209] and that were one to look at mainline Protestant denominations, even when congregations have been remaining open, they have been both experiencing a drop in attendance and youth participation and, in many cases, have shifted to part time pastors. This has had a definite impact upon those considering ordained ministry. Were one to explore the employment opportunities posted for mainline

---

209 They are also dealing with significant issues of division.

pastors, one would find an increase in those who would be
serving on a part time basis. This has all kinds of implications
in terms of career planning and its accompanying issue of
income within the profession of one's choice. As an important
side note, at the time of this writing, information has emerged
showing a considerable increase in the number of clergy either
leaving their churches or opting out of parish ministry [210] at
all. Much of this is attributable to the impact of the pandemic
on the life of local churches.

•   Consequently, it should come as no surprise that churches
    which are dealing with declining attendance, a drop in
    income, an aging population and the loss of a youth base
    are struggling with remaining open. This reality has caused
    incredible consternation among those long connected to
    the church who are troubled by the fact that current church
    realities just cannot compare to the "way things used to be."[211]

My Concerns

Yet having said this, I need to share some of my concerns:

•   First and foremost is my respect for the mainline traditions
    within Protestantism.
•   Along with that, as I have noted throughout this book,
    I am deeply concerned with the rise of the evangelical,
    nondenominational churches and how they approach Biblical,
    theological and social issues.

A True Story: the Good and the Bad

In my second year serving as a pastor at the church I served
most recently [212], an Episcopal church in the same town and just

---

210 Much writing has been done on this topic recently.
211 That well known cliché!
212 Grace Lutheran, Plainville, Connecticut.

a couple of miles away closed. One Sunday morning, a couple showed up at our church who were members of that congregation and who told me that they were now exploring possible options for a local church for them to be a part of going forward. This couple, I discovered, was deeply involved in the life of the Episcopal congregation that was integral to their spiritual lives.[213] They also had great respect for the priest who served as their pastor.

As it turned out, several other members of that congregation showed up as well and expressed the same thing. In this exploration process, I spent time meeting with individuals and explaining the similarities and differences between Episcopalians and Lutherans. I emphasized how these denominations had been working together closely and cooperatively for years. I shared the nuances of each church's theological positions and encouraged them to ask any question they wished, which they did!

The bottom line here is that within the next few months, five people from that local Episcopal church connected with and became members of our local church, a congregation of the Evangelical Lutheran Church in America. They went on to be active, dedicated members of our church and remain active participants in that wonderful faith community.

Glad as I was to serve in a church with such terrific people and cognizant of how Episcopal and Lutheran congregations had joined together in so many positive ways, I felt sad for the local Episcopal church and those who were so nurtured spiritually through their involvement in it. Coupled with that was my respect for the Episcopal tradition for a variety of reasons, dating back to when I was a teenage Roman Catholic seeking out options for my future life in organized Christianity.

SOME SUGGESTIONS FOR CONSIDERATION:

The underlying suggestion I would make is this:

---

213 This is mentioned in previous chapter.

I firmly believe that if at all possible, mainline churches should try their very best to do all that they can to remain open.

In addition, I would like to suggest as well that, within local communities and neighborhoods, these churches go out of their way to establish opportunities to interact with other mainline churches as well as faith communities within the Roman Catholic and Orthodox traditions through the following:

- Shared worship experiences- Revitalizing worship during the annual Week of Christian Unity [214] is a very good place to start.
- Shared educational programs which include both Bible study and the history/background of each other's denominations
- Shared youth ministry activities as I have exemplified in this book
- Shared engagement in projects for the betterment of their town /neighborhoods
- Shared promotion of musical concerts and performances and perhaps the possibility of performing plays together

Now, one could make a case that to do all of that, all we would need to do is close a church in the area and then have people attend another church. Apart from the fact that this may not work for some people what excites me is how shared learning and other activities among congregations from different denominational backgrounds could be a wonderful spiritual and educational experience with a lot of vitality and excitement attached!!

What do you think? Am I being naïve here? I am sure some would argue that I am! If you are having conversations about this book, in your church, your home, or both… please consider exploring this question!

---

214 I feel that churches should do all they can to revitalize this week which
   celebrates the importance of ecumenism within Christianity.

THE WAY THINGS WERE

Some would contend that this is not doable and that the simple fact is this: Certain congregations just must close. Why they would need to do so has many factors. These include:

- The cost of keeping the building up to par
- The opportunity to connect with another local congregation as those members of my former church have done
- A merging of congregations that could lead to churches with more active participants

AN INTERESTING INSIGHT

An insight worth thinking about and discussing may be found in an article to which I have alluded:

> *Too many churches are cluttered with all sorts of programs and activities that aren't really designed to form Christian identity and practice. Many of these are holdovers from previous eras. They may be meaningful to legacy members but not transferable to newer generations or diverse neighbors. We need to rediscover and reclaim the simple practices that Christians have always done—prayer, scripture study, service, reconciliation, Sabbath, hospitality, etc.—and make these the center of congregational life. Such disciplines must be expressed in forms ordinary members can practice in daily life throughout the week as they discern and join God's leading in their neighborhoods and spheres of influence.[215]*

There is a good deal of wisdom in the above quotation. I would add to this the following:

---

215 From the article *"Will the ELCA be gone in 30 years?"* September 5, 2019 published by Faith and Lead, a publication of Luther Seminary in Minnesota.

- *For the above to be achieved, individual congregations need not close.*

- *What is of great importance is engaging people to participate in dialogue with those in local churches who are part of a different denomination from their own. This dialogue can also entail participation in shared worship!*

IMPORTANT POINT

Having said all of this, the reality remains that some congregations WILL need to close for a variety of factors unique to them. I am not suggesting that no church ever needs to close!

However, if well planned out and structured, people from varied congregations and church traditions can benefit from interaction with each other on the level of worship, religious education and interpersonal dialogue. While closures may STILL, in particular circumstances, need to happen, they need not be normative.

An interesting article raises these points:

Unless a grain of wheat falls into the earth and dies, it remains just a single grain; but if it dies it bears much fruit (John 12:24).

Across the ELCA, closing congregations' assets are being used to support vibrant, ongoing ministries and new outreach initiatives.

In recent years the Nebraska Synod has creatively repurposed several congregations' properties. The synod sold St. James Lutheran's property in the small town of Edgar, Neb., to facilitate creation of a community center and coffee shop. In Omaha the former American Lutheran now houses Nile Lutheran Chapel, a thriving Sudanese community expected to become a new ELCA congregation.

A similar "mission restart" is afoot in Seattle, where Bethany Lutheran Church closed in 2016.Emmaus Table, an inclusive, intergenerational worshiping community grounded in Lutheran expression, has been developed by the Northwest Washington Synod. The community meets at Bethany's former building, now called

7400 Woodlawn and repurposed to connect and engage with its Green Lake neighborhood.

A Tigrayan congregation uses the building, along with a preschool and the Emmaus partner Community Loaves, which provides home-baked bread to area food banks.

In Milwaukee, Capitol Drive Lutheran Church gave its building to the Table, which is described as "an innovative synod-authorized ministry." The Table began offering worship services there this year. The building also houses a culinary school, a yoga studio and an art studio.

Similarly, after the merger of two congregations in Midland, Mich., the former building of St. Timothy Lutheran became a community literacy center.

When Grace Lutheran Church in Two Taverns, Pa., concluded its ministry, the funds were distributed to 10 agencies in the Lower Susquehanna Synod. Recipients were chosen carefully to carry forward Grace's historic commitments to serve youth, a local fire company, Scouting and several agencies that assist food-insecure and unhoused people.

Deborah McClellan, a deacon and the last rostered minister to serve at Grace, assisted the congregation in selling the church building to a startup funeral home that promotes green burial practices.

After First Lutheran Church of Glendale, Calif., closed, its property became the Lutheran Center, where the Southwest California Synod office shares space with an Episcopal seminary and continuing education center. And in Houston, the Gulf Coast Synod keeps its offices in a former congregation's building, out of which it hopes to start a worshiping community.

Many arms of the church remind us how important it is to have a will as we position our assets to serve family members and others after we die. Congregations must also contemplate a time when the doors must close and the lights are turned off one final time. Such planning might seem an act of faithlessness or throwing in the towel, but in truth it shows confidence in God's power to bring new life out of death. [216]

MY RESPONSE :

To be clear, the mainline church has an extremely important role in religious life as expressed in the overall life of the local community. The loss of mainline churches leaves a void in religious options and opens the door to even more possibilities of Christian religion being seen as expressed in conservative forms of Christianity.

While, unfortunately, some closures are inevitable, my view is that we need to do all we can to keep these mainline congregations alive.

This is important to me - and I would welcome your response! [217]

---

216 This is from the article "Church closures yield growth", found in the Living Lutheran magazine, October 12, 2022.

217 You may post on the Facebook page Robert LaRochelle. You may also use Facebook to send me a message or ask a question!

6

RECLAIMING CHURCH: YOUNG ADULTS AND ADOLESCENTS

Over these last few years, I have served in several mainline Protestant churches. In the recent decade, I have been pastor of three different congregations and also served a congregation as its pastor for three months when the pastor at that church took his sabbatical. In addition, I have visited many congregations and filled in as a supply pastor when their clergypersons were away on vacation or during those times when they were in the process of searching for a new pastor.

While each congregation is unique, all these mainline Protestant communities of faith had this fact in common:

If you were to look out into the congregation from my vantage point towards the front of that church, this is what you would see:

*   Most of those worship participants were men and women who would be considered as senior citizens or were at least on the brink of earning that status. This they shared with the pastor officiating at the service![218]
*   There were very few children in the pews in comparison to what one might have found a couple of decades earlier and definitely in comparison with what I had experienced in my years as a child growing up in my church.

---

218 Me!!

- While there were adults present who were in their 20's and 30's, there really weren't many.

Now, even though I, along with active members of those congregations, made extensive efforts to increase the numbers of participants from a younger demographic and even with the success of some of the initiatives we took, the reality remained that we were most definitely climbing uphill.

LET'S EXPLORE WHY

First, I would like to acknowledge that statistics are important. In fact, I have found over the years I have served both in the field of education and in church settings that presenting data to people is a very helpful and necessary thing. When one is examining data what is happening is that people are coming face to face with realities and the process of examination provides a great launching pad for further conversation and exploration.

Examining data helps to keep things realistic and provides a necessary resource for a good planning process! It can help avoid the often inevitable activity of protecting that which we do not want to lose. In this case, our church community and the building that has become an important part of our lives!

HOWEVER...

At the same time, there must be a balance. Bombarding people with statistics can, in some cases, be counterproductive. Nonetheless, it is important that pastors and others charged with church leadership take time to explore current trends in church attendance and participation. One of the benefits of doing this is that through this exploration, one might discover possibilities for what needs to be done within the congregation. Consequently, I would contend that data is important and that in researching and thinking through available data regarding the institutional church, we can get a good sense of reality and avoid interpretations that are driven by emotion or by the tendency to yearn for what used to be.

In short, good statistical information provides a necessary reality check!

SOME IMPORTANT FACTS

We need to start with some important basic facts:

The available data shows that over the last few years there has been a clearcut decline in overall church attendance. Here are some important statistics:

- In 2019, 34% of those connected with Christian churches attended worship services regularly.
- In 2021, the number dropped to 28%.
- Over that period, those who claimed that they NEVER attended worship services rose from 50 to 57%.[219]

It has been convenient for many people to cite the onset of the COVID-19 pandemic as the cause of this decline. HOWEVER, the reality shows that this decline was in process well before the pandemic struck. Significant studies which include important statistical data make this quite clear. While I do not want either myself or you, the reader, to get lost in a statistical quagmire, I DO think it is important to lay out some facts that are available through an exploration of significant data.

While one could explore many topics by reflecting on all of this factual, statistical information, what I would like to do here is examine the demographics involved in the matter of who attends worship services with some regularity:

A simple synopsis makes very clear that there has been a decline over the years in adolescent and young adult attendance. Some have referred to this fact as contributing to the "graying" of mainline congregations. Another way of putting this is to say that

---

219 Some details are accessible on the Lifeway Research site, including the article "Attendance Trends You Need to Know", February 2, 2022.

church attendance includes a great number of middle aged and older participants.

To lay this out simply and directly, here are some facts:

While there ARE children, adolescents and young adults who DO attend worship with some regularity, the numbers are down both from the heyday of church participation and even from what was happening in churches as recently as one or two decades ago.

WHAT DOES THIS LOOK LIKE?

Every mainline congregation is different and some I have known have been very good at integrating both adolescents and young adults into a congregation's overall life. However, based both on what I have read AND what I have experienced as a pastor, here is what I have discovered:

- Most attendees at worship come from a middle age to senior citizen demographic range.
- In most mainline churches as well as the Roman Catholic church, there has been a decline in youth ministry and the reality of nonexistent youth groups.
- While some churches have addressed ways to connect with young adults, with some exceptions, this has not been successful.
- Young adults as a demographic group are not really drawn to the mainline institutional church. Some changes in this may occur if they eventually raise children. However, that is not something of which one can necessarily be assured.

A PRACTICAL EXAMPLE

To be very direct and concrete about this, I would like to describe my own experience as a pastor over the last couple of decades in several mainline congregations I have served. I want to focus on what I have seen both in Sunday worship and overall church activity. I also want to note that during this time, I have taken some steps and developed some initiatives to address these issues, but, having said that, I also think it is important to describe the realities that I have seen which indicate that:

- Very few young adults or adolescents are in the pews during worship. The exceptions with respect to adolescents would be those who are there to fulfill a requirement of some sort as well as those dragged there by parents or other family members!
- New members of these churches primarily come from within the middle age/senior citizen range, with some exceptions.
- When I arrived at my most recent church pastorate, there were very few operative programs in that church either for youth or for young adults.
- A good number of people who might be intrigued by the possibility of attending worship as they have a deeply rooted spiritual sense do not find themselves accepted within established mainline churches. This could be with respect to the clothes they wear, their style of hair or beard, or the particular emotional difficulties they are experiencing. In every church I have ever served, I have had people drop by on Sunday morning not to go to worship but perhaps come by after church to have a conversation with the pastor. They needed the church but did not feel the church would be comfortable with them. Very sad!

In addition, these are two other important things that I have also observed:

- Older members of the congregation would love to see more young people in the pews as well as more youth involvement in the overall life of the congregation.
- Churches have tended to resort to strategies to build youth programs and engage young adults that are essentially INEFFECTIVE. While extremely well intentioned, for sure, they tend to include methodologies that do not resonate with current teens and young adults.

THERE IS AN ALTERNATIVE OUT THERE:

My experience has been that even in very small congregations, there are some young people who are of middle school and high school age. Some of you reading this may be *thinking "OK, but they are not at my church."* I understand where you are coming from as I have served in congregations where there were very few middle and high school youth in the pews. Having said this, as I have made some suggestions based on the assumption that in most congregations this is definitely a fact, I will also proceed to offer some suggestions in places where there really are none of or very few youth, for whatever reason!

WHEN A CHURCH HAS VERY FEW YOUTH WITHIN IT

It is important in this situation that the young people within the church be affirmed without being pressured. In other words, in the midst of the concern *that "we have to do something for our youth"* [220], it is also necessary to understand that young people have a lot of things going on at one and the same time. They have school commitments, outside activities, points of connection with friends and in many cases, jobs to which they must attend.

In these congregations with very few young participants, I nonetheless suggest that the pastor and Christian Education leaders be sure to structure programming for youth within the church AND to help find points of connection with other mainline Christian churches in their area. I do not think that overkill is required. Instead, it makes sense to have ongoing opportunities provided which, at the same time, are respectful of the other commitments young people have.

It seems to me that two things are needed, both at the same time:

1. The church needs to insure that opportunities exist for middle and high school youth within their congregation.

---

220 A common message to church leaders as conveyed by adults!

2. At the same time, adult leaders should be active helping to find those points of connection for these youth with other mainline churches. This involves adult leaders being willing to find ways to reach out to other churches with ideas for shared activities. These activities can be in the areas of shared conversations, interesting educational programming featuring discussions of relevant topics and establishing programs in which they can gather and have a good time. I would also suggest that pastors be involved in this process. This is best attained when pastors remain connected to other pastors in the area in which they serve.

3. *I strongly encourage youth leaders within congregations to do the following:*

4. If possible, be sure that a high school and middle school youth group exists. If the numbers are small, they might have to be combined and leaders will need to find a way for youth of different ages to work on projects together.

5. However, and this is important, even with small numbers in each age group, it is essential that churches offer opportunities geared to the different age levels.

6. No matter what other mainline churches happen to be doing or NOT doing, those adults engaged in youth ministry should make active attempts to reach out to youth leaders and pastors in other mainline churches within a reasonable geographic distance.

7. Most importantly, it is crucial that local mainline churches simply DO NOT GIVE UP on the importance of youth ministry.

Wherever possible, even when youth activity involves sharing programming with other churches, one has to be conscious of the "distance factor." The high probability is that those adults driving their daughters and sons to youth activities are really busy themselves is a simple reality.

When churches schedule activities to which youth of other churches are invited, they have to be very deliberate in how they develop their scheduling so as to make the events they offer a viable possibility for youth who may be gathering and who come from a variety of locations! Unfortunately, I have witnessed situations in which this was extremely difficult for many youth and their families.

THIS IS ESSENTIAL

While the pastor, with all her or his varied responsibilities, need not be the person to " run" the youth group, her /his support is essential, as well as is the pastor's availability to interact with young people.

There very well may be some situations where a pastor was once an active youth group leader. In that case, she/he could become a great resource for helping lay leaders build the program. Unfortunately, on occasion, I have witnessed some churches whose pastor has taken a completely "hands off" approach to youth ministry. Fortunately, that is not typical, yet, to be honest, I HAVE witnessed it!

Nonetheless, with all the varied responsibilities pastors have, it remains important that they provide support to those who may be willing to help with youth ministry and that they make themselves present to the young people who participate. This need not mean that they run the program but it does mean that they see it as integral to the life of the church and of importance to their youth, as well as the friends of their youth who may be drawn to the activities they sponsor.

NOT JUST ADOLESCENTS

The same methodology applies to developing programming for young adults who have found themselves connected in some way to the congregation. While youth ministry and young adult programming simply must be separate, some of the same principles apply in terms of structuring effective programming.

In Both Programs: Youth Ministry And Young Adult Ministry

In both programs, one of the things that is MOST ESSENTIAL is for leaders of the church, which most definitely includes the pastor, to be supportive of its importance AND for them to take the initiative to reach out to other mainline congregations in the area, many of whom might be caught up in lamenting that the "*way things used to be*" both for youth and young adults is simply not happening within their churches.

Some Examples

Here is where some of the more "conservative" churches offer some examples for "mainline" congregations. The Vox[221] churches which have popped up in many places in my native New England, provide great opportunities for young adults and parents, as do some of the structures developed in some Roman Catholic diocese. My issue with their efforts has less to do with their organizational structure which is most EFFECTIVE in a large number of circumstances. My biggest concerns center on the theology often espoused by those churches.

As a side note, as a resource for getting an up to date feel for the possibilities inherent in structuring a youth group as well as youth ministry's ups and downs, if you happen to ever read Jonathan Franzen's book *Crossroads*[222], while the book is not ABOUT mainline church youth ministry, you will see that it DOES provide a very realistic overview of many of the dynamics involved therein. It is a really good book!

To Be Honest

If we are being perfectly honest about the adult and youth ministry within the institutional church, we would have to admit that many evangelical churches, including the independent ones,

---

221 More about Vox is explained later in this book.!
222 I highly recommend this book!

have a rather high success rate in drawing young people, including young adults, into participation. In fact, in these congregations, when young adults are active in Sunday worship, it is not unusual for their children to find ways to participate simultaneously in church programming as well and to have significant times when they are drawn into leadership during the worship services of that church.

There is much to commend the structure of adult and youth programming in many of these churches. They have been extremely successful in filling the void in established religion that has been present in traditional mainline congregations. In many churches, they provide a safe environment for those young people drawn to them. At least they do so up to a point.

In addition, there are a good number of mainline churches which continue to go out of their way to offer youth opportunities. They are to be commended! They serve as examples of a church commitment to youth ministry which has faded away in all too many places.

To reiterate however, in my mind, the theology presented in youth programming in the conservative, evangelical wing of Christianity is quite questionable. In addition, I have concerns for what is happening in terms of programming for young people in many conservative leaning Roman Catholic churches. I wish to cite as an example an approach which is quite popular in the area of the country in which I live. While this church might not at this time be everywhere in the United States, this kind of church is found throughout the country.

To be specific, however, I am going to look at the programming offered by what is called the VOX CHURCH.[223]

BUT FIRST...

However, I need to be as clear as possible regarding the perspective from which I am coming. I admire many things about

---

223 See web site.

what Vox Church does. A look at their web site makes quite clear that there is a lot of positive activity going on, including significant outreach to those in need. However, I do have several concerns about these independent churches which I will explain in more depth below.

THE EMERGENCE OF CONSUMER CHRISTIANITY

Vox Church, along with many other independent churches to be found in North America, emerged out of what I would call a "breakaway tradition." [224] In fact, though it, along with other so called megachurches, came out of different strains within American Christianity, it does represent a breakaway from historic Catholicism, Orthodox Christianity and Protestantism. To explain this position, a brief review of religious history is needed.

CHRISTIAN RELIGIOUS HISTORY...
THIS IS IMPORTANT ...

One of the most important realities of which Christians need to be taught to be aware is a working knowledge of basic Christian history. This is important because considering the abundance of different Christian denominations, it is understandable that people might wonder why they pay allegiance to their church or denomination when there are so many different options out there.

Having taught Christian history in schools for several years and in educational forums in churches I have served, I would be the first to say that I can understand how people find it all quite confusing and complicated, deeming much of it all quite questionable. Part of the problem is that it is quite likely that in discussing religion, people are inevitably referencing the theological background which has formed their own church experience, an approach which could also be antithetical to other ways of experiencing Christianity and the church.

---

224 This includes churches whose leaders may have " broken away" from the
    mainline and have developed connections with other similar churches.

In A Nutshell...

As we know, the first established Christian church is what we call the Catholic Church, best known as the Roman Catholic Church. The Eastern Orthodox Church, known popularly as the Orthodox Church split from Rome as did many Oriental Christian churches at the Council of Chalcedon in AD 451. The Eastern Orthodox Church has become the dominant Christian denomination in many nations with a large number of followers today.

The Orthodox split from Roman Catholicism was a significant one. However, the break from Roman Catholicism which ultimately impacted the Western world even more was the Protestant Reformation which emerged in Europe and was established in the 16th century, with its driving force being the activity of Father Martin Luther, a Roman Catholic priest in Germany. In addition, John Calvin was a significant influence, as were others as well, including many whose names may not be terribly well known by most but which demonstrated significant impact.

In a nutshell, this split led to a variety of new religious denominations which in the United States has come to include those who would be known as Lutherans[225], Anglicans (or Episcopalians), Reformed Christians, Presbyterians, Methodists, Disciples of Christ, Mennonites and several other newly established Christian denominations. [226]

Christianity In America

When we look to the origins of Christianity in the United States, we see events such as Protestants coming over on the Mayflower and landing in New England, as well as extensive establishments of Anglican congregations throughout the colonies.

---

225 Inspired by the words and actions of Martin Luther.
226 Much of this research information with respect to historical facts is available in encyclopedias and in articles online. It would be a separate task to try to explain it all within the confines of this chapter and/or this book. Suffice it to say: It is both complicated AND worth exploring! I strongly suggest you consider doing so!

Over time, we would see that what would come to be known as the United States developed considerable religious diversity. We also become aware of the emergence of Christian denominations as having considerable impact as well.

While diversity in Christian religious practice was clearly present, American Protestantism was dominated by denominations, many of whom would proceed to establish both churches and schools. Depending upon sections of the country, the following churches established a plethora of Protestant congregations in the newly formed United States: Episcopal, Presbyterian, Baptist, Congregational, Methodist and several offshoots of each. A good number of long-standing prominent colleges came out of these church traditions.[227]

Over time, many Catholics traveled to the new world, and established churches, cemeteries, and schools.

CHRISTIAN EDUCATION IN AMERICAN CHURCHES

As they developed and grew, Protestant denominations and Catholic churches alike established schools on the primary, secondary and collegiate level. These schools included among them denominational seminaries. On the local church level, provision was made for insuring that young people were taught the fundamental tenets and unique positions found within their denominations and churches.

ESTABLISHED CHURCHES: WHAT DOES THIS HAVE TO DO WITH CHURCHES TODAY?

Current trends have shown both a reduction in the number of established mainline Protestant churches as well as Catholic churches in many areas. In addition, a good number of both Protestant and Catholic seminaries for training future clergy have closed

---

227 Though schools such as Harvard and Yale come readily to mind, there are many colleges and universities which grew out of a religious tradition.

as well [228] Historically, mainline Christian congregations have, over time, relied on rigorous, challenging seminary training for their clergy. Roman Catholics and Orthodox Christians have done so as well. Over the last few years, there has been a decline in available seminaries, and several have undergone closure. At the same time, the more conservative Christian churches have continued to offer training of some sort for potential preachers and pastors.

Historically, mainline churches have been led by pastors with a very strong, rigorous academic training in topics of Scripture, worship, church history and contemporary church trends, as well as through an intense program of Clinical Pastoral Education.[229] To be honest, the training grounds for conservative clergy do not provide the breadth and depth of this needed background. In addition, the colleges and universities established by Protestant denominations as well as Catholic colleges, including those established by the Jesuit order,[230] include some of the most distinguished academic institutions in the United States. Unfortunately, the quality and depth of the training offered to many evangelical, conservative clergy is lacking in many areas.

New independent Christian churches have been popping up all over the place. While they are affiliated with other congregations that share their theology, they are also disconnected from the mainline. While I knew this from my reading over the years, I first became really aware when my wife and I were down in the Carolinas and while being driven to see the sights of the area by my brother and sister in law whom we were visiting, we went down a

---

228 One example in New England is the Episcopal seminary near Boston. In addition, some denominational seminaries have sold their buildings while offering programs in conjunction with other seminaries.

229 Also known as CPE, this is an in depth program for prospective pastors which is centered on helping them develop skills in ministering to those with a variety of pastoral needs, including those who are dying and their families.

230 I attended one of them (Holy Cross) as an undergraduate and another (Boston College) when I earned my Master's degree in Religious Education. There are many Jesuit colleges throughout the United States.

highway where there was an incredible number of churches to be found on all sides of the road. What I noticed most was that in addition to some of the mainline churches, there were all kinds of others that could best be described as both independent and quite fundamentalist. An exploration of the educational background of those with the title pastor would indicate that these pastors really did not receive in depth training either in pastoral skills or in theology.

As an interesting and I hope worthwhile activity for those of you reading this book, I would suggest that you consider taking a drive and checking out the number of your churches in your area. As you write these down (not while you are driving as you should have someone in the car with you), be sure to notice the variety of denominational types that may be present in the area in which you live. It is quite likely that you will find a good number of churches, even in the small towns through which you might be driving.

Of course, you could do it more easily, I suppose, by just going to the Internet, but I think there would be something more interesting about just taking a ride. Of course, you could always add going out to lunch or getting some ice cream as part of your project!

Going back to a few years ago, there has been an explosion of these independent loosely affiliated churches up north as well. As I drive through the area in which I live, New England, I see them everywhere, including, as I previously noted, in the area in which I grew up, i.e. Putnam and its Eastern Connecticut surroundings. One very large church which is only a couple of miles from me in the town in which my wife and I live has taken over what used to be a popular wedding and banquet establishment and has now become a building housing a rather large evangelical church.

In addition, throughout the state of Connecticut and much of New England, there has been an explosion in what is known as the VOX churches. As I noted, I will be featuring some information about them in this section below whose purpose is to draw the distinction between Catholic, Orthodox and Mainline Christian churches and the phenomenon of evangelical, independent churches which are now quite visible in the communities that constitute our nation, all at a time when the mainline church is on the decline.

THE INDEPENDENT CHURCH

In providing information on this topic, as I noted above, I am going to feature what I know about the phenomenon of the VOX church. While all independent churches have their own unique approaches to church matters, the VOX model is indicative of what one would see in a wide variety of independent churches.

IMPORTANT NOTE: Many of these churches would argue that they are not independent but that they are connected to a denomination. I would contend that while there are definite points of connection, there is not the kind of focus one would find either in the theology or structure of mainline Protestant or Roman Catholic or Orthodox churches. For example, Roman Catholic, Lutheran, Orthodox, Episcopal, Presbyterian, Lutheran and Baptist churches, as well as many others too numerous to fully name right here, are each grounded in a theology that has evolved within their denominations. This theology is expressed in the structures of their churches, as well as their areas of focus.

As concrete examples in my own life, I would cite the Evangelical Lutheran Church of America (ELCA) and the United Church of Christ (UCC) which are both denominations in whose churches which I have served as a pastor.

AN INTERESTING EXAMPLE: THE VOX CHURCH

In the part of the country in which I live, while there is not the preponderance of independent churches one might find in the South, nevertheless, there is a growing number. One of the most popular in our area is the VOX church.[231] It exemplifies the approach found in most independent, evangelical churches. It identifies itself as being Biblically based and approaches the Bible as containing specific beliefs which constitute the doctrine of the

---

231 https://voxchurch.org/.

church. Its statement of faith is based on an evangelical theological approach which sees the words of the Bible as specific and direct and intended to be the guide for our lives. Its educational approach is really based on its statements and the faith they express.

Unlike mainline Protestantism and much of Catholicism, in its educational approach, it remains direct and simple. Whereas the approaches to Scripture found in mainline Christian denominations and taught in their seminaries are quite heavy with their complexity of theological backgrounds and trends, the approach found in the Vox church is much like that in most evangelical congregations. Simply put, one could say the approach is: *'This is what the Bible says... and that's that."*

The contrast here is with what you would find in exploring the theology and understanding of Scripture found in most mainline Protestant denominations and taught in their seminaries. It also reflects differences with how Catholics approach both doctrine and Scripture as well.

The following statements are from the web site of VOX Church:[232]

- We believe that the gospel of Jesus Christ is the most important truth in life. Jesus lived a perfect life, died a substitutionary death, and rose from the dead. This one truth changes every other part of life.
- Community is how God does things. We are told in scripture that God is one in essence and three in person (the Father, Son, and Holy Spirit).
- The heart of Vox Church is marked by a holy urgency. We believe that time is short, people need God, and he has called his church to be a voice. *The name "Vox" comes from the Latin word for voice, and we believe that God desperately wants to speak to those far from him and bring them close.* His primary method to do this is his church. As the people of God, we want to echo his truth in every corner of our world through sharing

---

232 From the web site cited previously.

the gospel, serving the poor, helping those in need, seeking the good of the city, partnering with other churches and organizations and participating in global missions is integral to the mission of this church.

- The death of Jesus Christ on the cross and his resurrection from the dead provide the *only* [233] way of salvation through the forgiveness of sin. *Salvation occurs when people place their faith in Christ as sufficient payment for their sin. Salvation is a gift from God and cannot be earned through our own efforts. The victorious work of Jesus on the cross provides eternal life and freedom from sin, lies, sickness, torment, and all the power of the devil.* (Isaiah 1:18; 53:5, 6; 55:7; Matthew 1:21; 27:22, 28:6; Luke 1:68, 69; 2:28, 32; John 1:12; 3:16, 36; 5:24; Acts 2:21; 4:12; 16:30, 31; Romans 1:16, 18; 3:23, 25; 5:8, 10; 6; 1 Corinthians 1:18; 2 Corinthians 5:17, 20; Galatians 2:20; 3:13; Ephesians 2:8, 10; Philippians 2:12, 13; Hebrews 9:24, 28; Revelation 3:20)

MY RESPONSE AND MY CONCERNS...

First, a short, cursory glimpse at this information could make it look very appealing, right? A focus on the Gospel, those communities called church, participation in the church's global mission and its service to those in need locally, are all worthwhile, wouldn't you say?

---

233 My point of emphasis. The implication in this statement raises legitimate questions regarding as to whether one NOT placing faith in the Resurrection of Jesus would be able to achieve salvation. I find this position problematic. It runs counter to the beliefs of many Christian churches and is described well in the theological works of Karl Rahner, especially with respect to his thinking regarding the " anonymous Christian". It also runs counter to decrees of ecumenism as developed in the Second Vatican Council. In my view, it is expressive of an approach that is problematic in evangelical Christianity. See my comments below.

HOWEVER, AND THIS IS IMPORTANT TO KNOW...

The statements of faith cited above are based on two significant approaches:

1. *A literalistic understanding of the Bible*
2. *An understanding of Christian doctrine that comes out of a conservative, evangelistic history within the Christian church*

This approach, not unique to the VOX church and found in a wide variety of evangelical churches and denominations, does not consider all of the variety expressed within the overall history of theology within Christianity. In saying this, I am not questioning the good intention of those who serve in leadership positions within this fairly new Christian community, In fact, in many ways they are to be commended.

Having said this, I would still maintain that there is more complexity within Christianity than one would find within this church body AND that this, along with many other conservative elements within Christianity, lacks a focus on social justice as an important expression of Christian faith and concentrates instead on issues of salvation in the context of life after death.

In addition, MANY of the churches within the conservative, evangelical wing of Christianity are very supportive of efforts that challenge the rights of homosexuals and transgendered individuals, including youth. They have also been involved in attacking curriculums in public schools, including what reading material should be banned.[234]

STATING THE IDEAL

To be clear and honest...

Churches such as Vox have provided excellent models for the structuring of youth ministry. They take this aspect of church ministry seriously and unlike many mainline Christian churches of long established denominations, they have NOT GIVEN UP on youth

---

234 To be clear, NOT ALL....

ministry. In their churches, it is quite vibrant and young people enjoy it very much. I would contend that there is much that mainline
churches could learn from the youth programming of some of these
newer faith communities, such as Vox and other more independent
evangelically driven churches. However, I would NOT include the
theology espoused as one of those important pieces of learning!

SUGGESTIONS FOR MAINLINE CHURCHES

Here is a simple summary of what I would then suggest for
mainline Christian churches:

1. Insure that a youth ministry program for both middle and
    high school students IS AVAILABLE in their congregations
2. Find ways to offer programs with other mainline churches, as
    well as with Roman Catholic churches---youth group meetings,
    retreats, etc.   Despite the conservative tilt in Catholicism
    over the last few years, I have remained convinced that this
    church, currently led by Pope Francis [235], continues to offer
    great potential in this area as well as in other areas of outreach
    and understanding of theology.
3. Place an emphasis on social outreach both within the church's
    youth group AND in its shared ministry with other youth
    groups of varied denominations.

While the specifics may vary from place to place and church
to church, the heart of the matter is quite basic :
CHURCHES... PLEASE... Do NOT give up on youth ministry!

---

235 Look for what I say about Pope Francis in the next chapter.

7

THE CATHOLIC CHURCH, RELIGIOUS EDUCATION. POPE FRANCIS AND THE FUTURE?

Perhaps you are wondering why I am veering off a bit from the overall direction of this book and presenting you a chapter that explores some facets of Roman Catholicism and the man who is serving as its Pope, also known as its Bishop of Rome,[236] Pope Francis. What might this possibly have to do with any of the topics and themes we have been exploring? I begin by stating something to you up front, something of which you are already aware if you have read some of my other books. Yet, in case you haven't, I think it important that I fill you in. If you have, here is a nice refresher!

At the time of this writing, I am now 70 years old. Have I mentioned this before?

For the first 45 years of my life, I was a Roman Catholic. I attended Catholic elementary school, a Catholic prep school, as well as a Catholic college and Catholic graduate school. In addition, I worked for thirteen years in Catholic education and was a Religious Education Director on both the diocesan level and for a couple of different Roman Catholic churches.[237] I address the specifics of my upbringing in some of my other writings, most thoroughly in my book *Crossing the Street.* [238]

236 The formal title for the Pope within Catholicism.
237 This is noted throughout this book.
238 Energion Publications.

The Roman Catholic Church played an important part in my life as well as in my religious formation. Though I ultimately opted to leave the Catholic Church [239], continue to hold it in great respect. While I am no longer active in the church and while I have significant differences both theologically and in terms of pastoral matters [240], I would never refer to myself as "anti-Catholic". Actually, quite to the contrary!

The Catholic Church, despite the leadership of a Pope who is considered to be more progressive than his most recent successors and has drawn the ire of many Catholic traditionalists [241], nevertheless, over these last few years has actually taken several conservative, traditionalist turns itself, first shaped by the pontificates of Popes John Paul II and Pope Benedict, but also continued through the years Francis has served as Pope, his time as Pope challenged by an active conservative Catholic backlash against him.[242]

THE CHANGES WITHIN CATHOLICISM

In exploring changes that have taken place in the Roman Catholic Church, we need to compare what has come out of the most recent Catholic pontificate, that of Pope Francis, with what the church experienced under the leadership of Popes John Paul II and Benedict.

TWO SIGNIFICANT REALITIES

To delve into these topics, it is important that we begin by citing two very significant occurrences within Roman Catholicism over these past few years:

---

239 I left Catholicism, not the church. Clear distinction!
240 How clergy approach issues. e.g.: Annulments, marriage prep, etc.
241 Please see the writings of Peter Wolfgang. Despite my significant differences of opinion with him, I refer to his extensive postings of conservative Roman Catholic positions with great frequency.
242 This has become increasingly problematic, in my view. Their positions can be found on many conservative Catholic web pages.

1. There has been a tremendous decline in the number of priests serving in the Catholic Church.
2. There has been a significant drop in the number of Catholic parishes and Catholic schools. This has led not only to many church closures but also to many mergers and the assignment of priests and deacons to more than one congregation.

With these realities have also come the following:

1. There has been an increase in conservative, traditionalist Catholic priests, now trained in more conservative seminaries than those trained in the time of Vatican II and several of the years that followed it [243].
2. The Catholic Church has experienced a decrease in distinguished progressive Catholic theologians.
3. Concurrently, there has also been a decrease in progressive Catholic laypersons studying in Catholic graduate school programs, including programs leading to degrees in the field of Religious Education.
4. There has been a noteworthy shift in the seminaries that have been preparing future priests, in particular with their study of theology and church law.
5. There has also been a noteworthy decline in a more progressive approach in the training of Permanent Deacons.
6. Religious orders of sisters have experienced significant decline over the last several decades, beginning in the 1960's.
7. Catholic "lay ministry" has taken a significant conservative turn.

THE WAY WE WERE

In June of 1989, in the Cathedral of St. Joseph in Hartford, Connecticut, I was ordained to the Roman Catholic Permanent Diaconate. After lying prostrate before the altar in this vast cathe-

---

243 This is due to decisions made by some rather conservative Bishops in many dioceses.

dral of the Archdiocese of Hartford, with hands placed on my head and words spoken by the Archbishop, I became what is known as a "Permanent" Deacon. Within Catholicism, the Diaconate is an ordained clergy position, one of the three ordained ministries of bishop, priest and deacon.

In the next few years following my ordination, it was my privilege to serve in my local Catholic parish, to preach with considerable frequency and to participate in baptizing a large number of children, as well as several adults and older youth as well.

At the time I was ordained, our diocese, the Archdiocese of Hartford, had an excellent four year program of preparation for the Permanent Diaconate. Its bishop, Archbishop John F. Whealon, was a distinguished Biblical scholar who taught at an interdenominational seminary in Hartford [244] and was extremely conversant in both Biblical languages and content. Those of us preparing to serve in the Diaconate were most privileged to have been taught by him. When I first read about Archbishop Whealon years prior, I was somewhat less than impressed. As I got to know him as my teacher and had the opportunity to engage in many conversations with him, I discovered that I was quite wrong. While I certainly did not agree with him on everything and while I was troubled by the closures in Catholic high schools that he initiated [245], there was MUCH that I respected in this man which I never had thought would ever happen!

In addition, the Permanent Diaconate program was led by two ordained married deacons, both of whom had a considerable amount of experience, with one of the men being on a unique, groundbreaking ministry team consisting of a priest, a deacon and a lay woman, all assuming significant ministry responsibilities within their parish.[246]

---

244 This was known as Hartford Seminary.
245 Including South Catholic in Hartford, which my wife attended and from which she graduated.
246 St. Elizabeth Seton Church, Rocky Hill, Connecticut.

The courses which I took in this program were taught by excellent teachers and scholars. Retreat experiences that were part of our training were excellent as well. At one point, deacons and deacon candidates were offered the opportunity to attend an excellent in person program offered by the distinguished theologian, Rev. Richard McBrien, who I had also been privileged to have as one of my teachers in my Master's program at Boston College years prior. I was very disappointed that we did not have a higher attendance at this program as I felt Permanent Deacons, most of whom did not have college or graduate school backgrounds in theology, really could have benefited from hearing this incredible theologian.

In addition, it is important to note that many of the parishes within the Archdiocese were staffed by excellent pastors who had received outstanding seminary training, many during the time period of the Second Vatican Council. Priests from our Archdiocese also were able to take advantage of the outstanding program offered for priests at the University of Notre Dame and taught by renowned theologians.[247]

AND THEN...

It is important to state that Archbishop Whealon would most certainly not be seen as a theological liberal. In fact, in many ways, he was quite traditional. As a matter of fact, before I first got to know him as my teacher, my knowledge of him from afar did not impress me at all. I saw him as a rather conservative bishop serving a church that had emerged from Vatican II and most assuredly needed to make a lot of changes.

Before I began my Diaconate training, because of my working as a Religious Education Director and Youth Minister in local parishes within the Archdiocese, I was offered the opportunity to attend an event called the New England Conference of Religious Education, attended by many priests, sisters, educators, volunteers,

---

247 My pastor, the late Catholic priest, Father Daniel Sullivan, took part in this. My oldest son and I had the opportunity to visit him there when we attended a football game at Notre Dame.

and Directors of Religious Education from throughout the six New England states.

One of the speakers at the Conference was someone I knew and respected. When I was talking with him, a definite Catholic liberal, he told me how much he respected Archbishop Whealon. I have to say I was somewhat surprised but I both knew and liked this speaker!

As it turned out, as I was taking a look at some of the displays to be found on the various tables that we participants could peruse at this event, I happened to be alone at one of the tables and alongside the Archbishop. I noticed two things about him that impressed me:

•   He was genuinely interested in the material displayed on these tables.
•   He was very low key and kind.

That brief contact indicated something to me that I discovered in the years when I came to know Archbishop Whealon. Yes, he was instinctively conservative, no doubt about it. However, he had both a great respect for Biblical and theological scholarship and He also had a gut level awareness that the post Vatican II church had to be open to change. In addition, He had a strong belief in making both ecumenical and interfaith connections and participated in a weekly seminar in which Catholic, Protestant and Jewish scholars studied Scripture in the languages of the Biblical texts.[248] In addition, He supported innovation in parishes within the Archdiocese he served, best exemplified by the building and staffing of a new parish in a suburb south of Hartford.[249] The very fact that the Archbishop was behind the idea of building a new parish is rather amazing considering what we have seen since in the reality found in the number of Catholic churches which have either closed or merged with others, offering limited services in their particular location. As you can tell from what I have written, I would never

248 At Hartford Seminary.
249 St. Elizabeth Seton, Rocky Hill, Connecticut.

label Archbishop Whealon as a liberal or progressive. However, my admiration for him grew from that day forward. I came to admire the way in which he would both praise and defend Father McBrien, whose writings were facing considerable criticism from the ever growing Catholic right wing, which by the time he came to speak to the deacons, were already making their criticisms of Father McBrien so well enough known that the turnout of those ordained to the diaconate who had the opportunity to hear Father McBrien speak was ridiculously low. *In my view, this was one of the greatest theologians in the Catholic Church and people in ordained positions were passing up the opportunity to learn from him.*

To be clear, the Archbishop had his flaws. As was the case with many bishops at that time, some of his decisions, especially regarding what to do with certain priests, fell quite short of the ideal.

Archbishop Whealon died in 1992. His funeral, which I attended along with other clergy of the Archdiocese, had an interesting, controversial footnote. Our state's Governor was Lowell Weicker, who was both an Episcopalian and a divorced man. Governor Weicker had a great respect for the now deceased Archbishop, and at the time in which people were invited to come forth and receive Communion, that is exactly what he did. In keeping with the spirit of the Archbishop, the priest distributing gave the Governor the element of bread.

I am not saying that the Archbishop would have done the same. He was not one to flout church rules. However, I CAN say that there was something about the Archbishop's heart that connected with our Governor's experience of knowing him. There is no doubt in my mind that our liberal Protestant Governor felt something was very special in the life of this conservative Archbishop of a church to which the Governor did not belong! I will never forget that funeral as long as I live. Truth be told, I was rooting quietly for Governor Weicker when I saw him emerge from his pew and move forward to share in Communion.[250]

---

250 To be honest, even on that day, in conversations with several attendees and in reading about the funeral, one would get the sense that a good

The words of the hymn say it all, in my mind and my heart:

One Bread, one Body, one Lord of ALL
One cup of blessing which we bless
And we, the many, throughout the earth,
We are one body in this one Lord [251]

THERE IS MORE TO THE STORY

While I liked and respected Archbishop Whealon, I must be honest and say that all was not perfect in the Archdiocese he served:

- In his final few years, news began to spread about the clergy sexual abuse crisis in the church. This included breaking knowledge about priests in the Archdiocese of Hartford.
- As a result of financial difficulties, the Archdiocese began the painful process of closing Catholic schools, including the one that my wife attended, a school that was held in high esteem for its academics and its spirit.[252]   As one who served several years as a teacher at a Catholic high school, I have found the closure of Catholic schools to be very troubling. My experience has been that Catholic schools provided a wonderful option for young people.
- The number of new seminarians was on the decline. The types of seminaries they were sent to for training were of a more conservative, traditionalist variety. This trend started to take shape after Archbishop Whealon had died.
- Catholic elementary schools were gradually engaged in the process of potential closure. Many outstanding schools that

---

number of Catholics were troubled by the fact that this divorced, Episcopalian Governor had received Communion in a Catholic cathedral!

251 One Bread, One Body is a well known contemporary Christian hymn. It is used in many congregations, Protestant and Catholic. It was written by John Foley.

252 South Catholic High School, Hartford, Connecticut.

played an important role in many communities ceased to exist. This has left a gap in educational alternatives for young people.

- The Archdiocese was about to lose a lot of money because of the many issues with which it was dealing.

To be honest, this was not unique to the Archdiocese of Hartford. In fact, the example of the sex abuse crisis with which most people were familiar took place in an ever-growing number of Catholic dioceses.

AS A RESULT

The death of Archbishop Whealon, coupled with the changes in his Archdiocese close to the time of his death, was part of a trend that virtually exploded beyond these Connecticut boundaries. The Catholic Diocese which, while most certainly not alone, nonetheless had the most attention cast upon it was up the road in the Archdiocese of Boston.[253] This trend became part of many other Roman Catholic settings as well.

In addition, the decline in priests, coupled with the new conservative wave in the church triggered by the election of Pope John Paul II, had several important effects. Among the many were these:

- There has been a noteworthy decline in church attendance.
- What has emerged is a trend toward papal appointments of very conservative bishops in the many dioceses throughout the world.
- Priests have had to undergo the experience of having their time split up between parishes they have been serving. This is due to the significant drop in seminarians preparing for the Catholic priesthood. At this time in which I am writing this book, this has certainly reached incredible proportions.
- There has been a drop in financial income which had an impact upon the ability of parishes to hire Directors of Religious Education who had graduate school background.

---

253 This was as a result of the sex abuse crisis.

- The church has experienced a movement toward a more conservative theology and return to several traditional religious practices that had been put on the back burner over the Vatican II years. This also had a major impact on the what and the how of Catholic school teaching. Let's just say that I am quite convinced that how I taught in a Catholic high school in the 80's would not be something I could do in these years when Pope John Paul and the conservative bishops he appointed were in charge.
- There has been a closure of respected seminaries and the deliberate intent of diocesan bishops to send seminary candidates to more conservative establishments.
- The church has experienced a halt on fresh theological thinking. Interestingly enough, this has occurred within the papacy of Pope Francis who is noteworthy for producing significant and challenging encyclicals, often inspired by current realities such as the environmental crisis. This spirit of Francis has not permeated the work of many church leaders.
- There has been a decline in Catholic Church participation in ecumenical events and worship with their Protestant neighbors.
- In addition, the church has witnessed a slowdown in any effort to allow for married priests.
- There has been a decline in the acceptance of ministry by women [254] and a halt to serious conversations about women's ordination and other roles of leadership.
- The church has undergone a newborn conservative alliance forged between Catholic leaders, Catholic organizations and the Republican Party. This was quite ironic considering the historic linkage of Catholic Democrats and immigration over several decades.
- In the Archdiocese of Hartford, as an example, there has been a major drop in the quality of materials offered by

---

254 Fortunately, the newly established church in Rocky Hill, CT. had a leadership team of which a laywoman was a member. She shared in the leadership of this parish. This was thanks to Archbishop Whealon!

the Archdiocese, including the elimination of the Catholic Transcript from its status as a weekly newspaper and its movement toward a monthly magazine style filled with much traditionalist theology. *This has left virtually no room for the dialogue that marked this important resource for Catholics in the Archdiocese, as well as for those of other faith traditions who sought to learn more about Catholicism. In my mind, one of its finest weekly pages in this excellent diocesan newspaper included the juxtaposition of Father McBrien's article with that of the more conservative scholar, Father David Liptak. This always struck me as a part of the publication that offered valuable material for study and for conversation!*

THERE WAS SOME GOOD NEWS

Despite the reversals described above and the pressures with which many Catholic educational institutions were under, several prominent Catholic colleges and universities have retained their openness and their commitment to academic freedom.

Foremost among these schools were those sponsored by the Jesuits. I would cite the theological faculties in places such as Holy Cross,[255] Georgetown and Boston College [256] as examples. I do so, however, with a recognition that the approach found in the study of Religious Education when I was student at Boston College in the 1970's has since taken somewhat of a more moderate turn. When I look back at my own experience in that program, I think of the professors who taught me and the progressive approaches they took in Catholic theology. In addition, other Catholic colleges such as the University of Notre Dame have also retained their openness. At one point, in fact, Notre Dame came under fire for welcoming

---

255 My alma mater.
256 Where I received a Master's degree.

Governor Mario Cuomo, a lifelong Catholic who advocated legalized abortion, to deliver a major address on campus. [257]

CATHOLIC RELIGIOUS EDUCATION AND YOUTH MINISTRY

There was a while, not long after the Second Vatican Council, when religious education in the local Catholic parish was both vibrant and growing. Here are some of the signs of this growth:

- Workshops for volunteers, including training in the Bible
- Good resources
- Creativity
- Vibrant Catholic high schools

Yet not too far along during the pontificate of Pope John Paul, things began to change dramatically.

- On the diocesan level came a change in the resources used for Religious Education classes on both the parish and Catholic school level. Whereas many previous Catholic educational texts encouraged thought and discussion regarding doctrines, dogmas and decision making, new text materials emphasized specific acceptance of church teaching. Religion teachers in Catholic high schools were REQUIRED to abide by these requirements. By this point, I had left the church - BUT...
- Coupled with this was the clear message being sent from the Vatican that several areas in which many Catholics were advocating for change were retrenching with the message becoming quite clear that these preferred changes were simply not going to happen. There was a tightening up in terms of religious education as mentioned above, as well as with respect to the issue of birth control. It was during this period in the United States that Catholic bishops began showing sympathetic allegiance to Republican politicians. It was becoming common

---

257 In this speech, Governor Cuomo made a case for a pro choice position on the issue of abortion.

as well to read about bishops overtly criticizing Democratic politicians who took pro choice approaches to the abortion issue. Gone was the "seamless garment" [258] approach that marked the ministry of Archbishop Bernardin in Chicago. Gone also was the healthy exchange of ideas found in many diocesan publications.

- On the scene instead would be found a bevy of activities rarely appearing in the days after Vatican II. These included:
- New, more traditionally based religious education materials.
- A reviving of Catholic practices including novenas,[259] Benediction of the Blessed Sacrament and Mary crownings, language changes in worship not reflective of current theological language.
- Changes in the liturgy as noted earlier in this book.

FRANCIS AND THE RISE OF THE CATHOLIC RIGHT

In the epilogue to the second edition of my book *Crossing the Street* [260], I explore the papacy of Pope Francis in considerable detail. I encourage you to consider reading that section. While I do not want to be excessively repetitive in this book, there IS something that I would like to state:

I greatly admire Pope Francis. There are many reasons for this:

- *He conveys a strong sense of openness to others.*
- *He is an excellent thinker and writer.*
- *His sermons (homilies) are outstanding. I always look forward to hearing his Christmas Midnight Mass message each year.*
- *He exudes great warmth.*
- *He has shown some significant progressive tendencies which have most certainly annoyed the Catholic Right.*

258 This emphasized the commonality people shared with one another. As a result of this, ALL were to be respected and treated fairly!
259 A novena is an experience of prayer recited over a period of several days, usually nine or more.
260 Noted in previous footnotes.

- *He is a man of deep prayer and is immersed in Ignatian spirituality, which I respect deeply.*
- *He is very nonjudgmental.*

Having said that, I have some concerns.

In fact, my main concern is my belief that when his time as Pope is ended, he will have missed out on the opportunity to make significant changes within the church. Please do not get me wrong here! I admire his approach to people and his openness to those from different religious traditions. I am particularly impressed by the way in which he has not let President Joe Biden's pro choice political positions lead him to denying the president Communion. This runs quite contrary to what we have seen in the ministry of many other Catholic bishops. I am also deeply grateful for his support of the Jesuit Father James Martin in his outreach to the LGBTQ community! Father Martin has been the recipient of unnecessary attacks on his theology and character from the Catholic right wing!

Pope Francis is an intelligent and kind man as well as an outstanding role model for pastoral leadership in the institutional church.

Unfortunately, it is quite possible that his time as Pope will come to an end with opportunities for even more significant changes being passed by as a result of his inaction. In the interest of straightforward honesty, I need to state that his inaction in these areas reflects his honest, sincere beliefs regarding what He should be doing in his leadership role. I respect that. Nonetheless, despite my great respect for the person he is and my deep appreciation for his homilies, encyclicals, statements and ways in which he treats people, I respectfully disagree with the following as I am concerned that this wonderful man has missed some great opportunities.

SPECIFIC CONCERNS

As I noted above, my underlying concern is that good and wonderful as he is, he has simply not gone far enough!

I cite these concerns:

- I truly wish that in this pontificate, he would have eliminated the mandate in favor of priestly celibacy. *I know a good number of wonderful priests who "left the priesthood" so that they could be married.*
- I would have liked it if Pope Francis opened the door for women to be ordained to BOTH the diaconate and the priesthood. *As someone who belonged to an organization supporting the admission of women to the Catholic priesthood since the early 1970's, I have found this delay and eventual absence to be troubling.*
- I wish he would have written an encyclical following up on *Humanae Vitae* and opening up the Catholic Church to accept contraception.
- I would have liked for him to be a stronger advocate for separation of church and state. While respecting his position on abortion, I wish he would have framed it within the context of legal decision making in pluralistic societies.
- I wish he had found a way to return the texts of the liturgy of the Eucharist to what was offered after Vatican II and wish he would not have allowed the texts of pre-Vatican II worship to be reintroduced in the liturgy. [261]
- I wish he would have found a way to eliminate the annulment process.[262]
- I wish he would have exerted more influence in his contacts with bishops to renew seminary life and support providing seminarians with theology inspired by Vatican II.
- I wish he would have encouraged local dioceses to upgrade the quality of messages communicated in their newspapers and magazines.

---

261 I find some of these changes to be extremely problematic.

262 To be honest, I have real issues with this process and speak from the experience of having helps several couples obtain annulments so they could be " legally" married within the Catholic Church. I did that when I was serving as a Deacon in the Catholic Church.

- While his respect for all persons regardless of sexual orientation has been commendable and refreshing, his reference to immorality as applicable to homosexuals is quite troubling.

LOOKING AHEAD

When I was young, the Catholic Church was a vibrant part of my life. For many reasons described in my writing, that has changed. Nonetheless, I will always respect it and seek ways to communicate to others the values to be found in so many of the ways in which it expresses Christian faith.

The Catholic Church provided me with a religious foundation, a strong one at that. Though over the years, I have had differences with many of its practices, I will ALWAYS be grateful for my Catholic experience.

The unfortunate thing is that I continue to be sad as well. I am sad that a church with such a great history has been viewed with disrespect by so many. I am sad that this church which experienced all of the changes found in the 1960's and 70's, has failed the challenge to face the future boldly and has found itself wallowing in much of the downside that has constituted its past.

Sad though I may be, I also get it. Yet, in getting it, I yearn for the days of a revitalized Catholicism, one that can engage in worthwhile dialogue and practice with other communities of faith in our shared Christian tradition.

I will end this commentary by invoking the words of John Lennon and editing them just a tad. They are words that speak of living out ideals, ideals that undergird so much that fills our life, including all of the what and the why of that which we call "our faith".

"You may say that I 'm a dreamer, but I'm not the only one"... I hope.[263]

---

263 From the song *Imagine* by John Lennon

8

RECLAIMING SPIRITUALITY

While there is much involved in developing meaningful programs within church congregations, as we have seen throughout these last few chapters, when all is said and done and push comes to shove, effective worship within the community of faith is something that needs to be of significant relevance and at the center of overall church planning.

To be clear, the purpose of effective worship is NOT to put on a good show for the congregation. However, poor worship leadership with music that does not touch the heart, a supposed variety which does not take into account different ways that individuals worship, an approach to prayer that does not seem relevant to real life and cliché ridden messages or messages delivered ineffectively get in the way of what is intended to be a meaningful spiritual experience, one that touches one's mind, spirit and body (More about that later).

In my view, it is nothing short of ESSENTIAL that worship leaders in congregations seek to develop ways of worship that connect with the spirituality that ought to be at work within the worship experience.

At the heart of all worship experiences is the expectation that, on some level, the one worshiping will get the sense that she/he is in touch with that which is "greater than all but present in each."

[264] Each particular religious tradition offers ways of drawing this out of those who gather for worship.

Unfortunately, there is an alternative "flip side" to all of this. For many attendees of church worship, the experience is that of a sense of rote responsiveness to familiar worship movements. *As an outgrowth of what might very well be poor theological teaching, it is very easy for worship language to be rote and repetitious.* Such is the formula for a less than ideal worship experience.

Ultimately, good worship is centered on these four elements:

1. Variety within the worship experience
2. Clear, concise, meaningful preaching
3. Music that touches the heart and mind
4. A clear relevance to the experience of worship in making a positive impact on everyday life

VARIETY WITHIN THE WORSHIP EXPERIENCE

Some students of good worship might very well make the case that there is something highly worthwhile about repetition in worship. Speaking only for myself here, I would say that while at worship, there *are* certain songs, prayers, or chants to which I look forward and which move me in a prayerful direction. In this regard, the act of repetition is definitely most effective!

I have had the fortunate experience of having both worshiped and led worship within a variety of denominational approaches to liturgy. Consequently, I have learned that there is some music that puts me in the right spiritual mood.

Nonetheless, I would also say that in some cases, repetition of unvaried prayers, songs and chants can feel like nothing more than going through the motions. A good deal of the blame for that, of course, would come back to me and deservedly so. It is important for someone

---

264 This is a quotation from the late Unitarian minister and author, Rev. Dr. Forrest Church. It appeared in much of his writing.

at worship to "clear one's mind" so to speak as one goes through worship's various phases.

Consequently, it is important that churches pay careful attention to developing good liturgy that speaks to people at different levels and that really helps one tune into a meaningful spiritual experience.

It is also important, in my view, that adolescents within a congregation have opportunities to experience worship that addresses their lives as young people. This would mean that worship leaders should have an openness to musical variety.

MUSIC AND WORSHIP

Beginning in the 1960's, many communities of faith, both Protestant and Catholic, began incorporating meaningful so called "secular music" [265] into the experience of worship. It was not unusual in Catholic high school or college worship or in the "Youth Masses" that were popular in some Catholic parishes for people to sing music that consisted of important themes related to such matters as human relationships, justice, and peace, rather than music more commonly used from traditional Catholic hymnals. In addition, there was significant growth in church music that came from Roman Catholic sources. [266]

Over time, new music written and sung by Catholic groups such as the monks of Weston Priory and St. Louis Jesuits added great variety to the celebration of the Eucharist [267] in Roman Catholic churches. Many of these so-called new hymns have gone on to become both Catholic classics and have made their way into Protestant hymnody as well. [268]

---

265 A term for music which is "not religious" in nature. Some, myself included, would contend that some "secular music" expresses religious themes and convictions. Though not alone, Bob Dylan's work is an example of this.

266 See examples below

267 Holy Communion

268 One can find many of these hymns in current Protestant hymnals.

Some music used in 1960's music was of the "secular variety" and while incorporated into church worship has tended to fade away in the years since the halcyon days of that time.

In some Catholic college and high school settings, it was not unusual to hear a secular song at a celebration of the Eucharist.[269] I will never forget a wedding ceremony I attended where the couple processed out of church together with the congregation singing *"Up, up and away in my beautiful balloon"*. [270]

At our wedding in 1980, a wedding held within the context of a Roman Catholic Mass and concelebrated [271] by three Catholic priests, the songs sung included popular music such as *"Longer Than"*,[272] and several others not found in Roman Catholic hymnals [273], all in the presence of these priests who were concelebrating the ceremony and who stated no objections to the use of so-called "secular music".[274] This wedding celebration was approved in advance by the pastor of that parish, a priest of the Archdiocese of Hartford, Connecticut.

This was all in contrast to something I experienced years later as I served as Deacon at a wedding Mass where I officiated at the exchange of vows. During one of the solos, the priest who was sitting in a chair next to me expressed his anger at a solo that was being sung which came from the soundtrack if a popular secular musical. I whispered to him that this was a decision the couple made and I thought it was wonderful!

---

269 This would be a song that would be from a realm outside of "sacred music.".

270 Obviously, a secular song!

271 A term used for when ordained priests lead worship together.

272 A song which was popularized by Dan Fogelberg.

273 It was wonderful and meaningful music both to my wife and to me!! I would really contend that it was quite religious in its expression!

274 I struggle with the use of the term "secular". As I see it, the sacred can most definitely be experienced in the experience of so – called secular music, poetry, literature and film. I find the dichotomy between secular and sacred to be problematic.

THE STYLE OF LITURGY

At the time we were married and in the preceding period in which we attended college, it was quite typical for those presiding at Catholic worship to include a variety of possible options for prayers and words used during the celebration of the Eucharist. Books published by Catholic publishers that focused on worship options emphasized variety in methods of worship.

WITHIN YOUTH MINISTRY

A distinctive style of youth group meeting evolved through the 1960's and into latter years. Within the Catholic church this emphasized an approach wherein young people at youth group meetings felt comfortable personalizing topics and discussions, engaged in an openness regarding their opinions and shared in opportunities for prayer services and the celebration of Communion, which was open, inclusive and included a wide variety of possibilities involving a range of readings and selection of music.

Many years later, these kinds of innovations had been back-tracked and were unusual to witness within the Catholic experience of youth ministry. For many years, I led youth group retreats, both overnight and in a church or other setting for a briefer period.[275]

The usual formats for these retreats consisted of:

The participants would sit in a circle. This would most often be on the floor. This setting was quite important to those who were participating.

A leader (which could also include youth leaders who were quite familiar with the format of these meetings)) would put out some opinions on a topic, either personal or of broader significance, with a discussion to follow facilitated by the youth group member. As the adult leader, I would be responsible for raising some questions and helping to facilitate the conversation as needed.

---

275 In the Diocese of Providence, my Christian Leadership class and serving as a youth minister in several churches.

Time was also taken up in these meetings by having conversations about ways that this youth group can engage in reaching out and supporting meaningful causes, including those necessary in this community.

Prayer time in the circle consisted of heartfelt personal prayer, the opportunity to pray in silence and concluding with some meaningful music. This ranged from music that was known in contemporary church services, as well as new music such as Michael Smith's *"Friends are Friends Forever."* [276] The musical experience was a culmination of the overall thrust of the typical youth group meeting of that day.

While serving as a Catholic youth minister, there were occasions when I arranged for our parish priests to come and preside at a Eucharist (Mass) for the young people participating in a retreat. In other situations, I arranged for a Communion service to be led by someone who was not a priest, in this case, me. Note: This service did NOT include the consecration [277] of the elements of bread and wine. In keeping with Catholic theology and law, the element(s) shared would have already been consecrated in a Mass presided at by a priest.

Over time, between overseeing and helping to structure youth group meetings in churches and in a variety of other settings [278], I was very pleased with the impact this experience had on many young people within the group. I have even read recently about some of its positive value in a column from one of my most active youth group members and leaders, a man deeply involved in conservative Roman Catholic causes, who discovered great merit and value in the youth group experiences of his day, in spite of his perception of the approach of the group's leader, i.e. me.[279]

---

276 A highly popular youth group song!
277 The Catholic term for the elements of bread and wine becoming the " real presence' of Christ in the celebration of the Eucharist (Holy Communion).
278 In my Christian Leadership class
279 See his comments below

Here are some thoughts on this topic as offered by Peter Wolfgang and noted in two columns he has written:

Soon a youth group started at my childhood parish and my 17-year-old self fell under the sway of the youth minister.[280] *He was a charismatic fellow, a Democratic activist who was a dissenter on all the usual issues except for abortion, and by the end of the year I was too.*

ALWAYS THAT TUG

And yet, there was always that tug. That little voice inside my head saying, "This is not right. This is not what you know to be true."

I was one of the youth leaders, tasked with coming up with topics for the next meeting whenever my turn came up. The youth group was social justice-oriented — visits to soup kitchens and so forth — and my two previous topics had been focused on contemporary issues.

But when my next turn came up, I wanted to talk about Heaven, Hell, and Purgatory. I led a discussion on how the choices we make in this world, our personal sins, can have eternal consequences. My teenage peers had, like me, been catechized by the inadequate CCD classes of the 1970s and 80s. But unlike me, they had not been exposed to Our Lady of Fatima. They seemed to be hearing about the possibility of eternal damnation for the first time.

The youth minister, clearly uncomfortable with the topic, assured them that they need not fear. God loved them and they were all going to Heaven.[281] *The message of Fatima was outdated. We knew better now.*

---

280 He was referring to me here.

281 I am quite certain my thoughts on this were either misunderstood or that I did not make them clear. I certainly made no assurances about the afterlife. I know that I was coming from the position that faith in the events of Fatima were not required to enter eternity and were also not comparable or on the plane of accepting specific doctrines of the Roman Catholic Church. This response actually speaks to the need for teachers of religion to explore matters in depth, not merely on the surface. That would include me in this case.

(A teacher at the local Catholic high school, he later left the Church to become a Congregational minister.) [282]

MY RESPONSE:

To this day, I have very fond memories of this member of my youth group and of that overall youth ministry experience. Over the last couple of years, Peter and I have stayed in regular touch. When COVID began to lift, we enjoyed going out to lunch together. He has also reviewed a couple of my books and gave his usual honest insights into what I wrote. [283]

While we approach many religious issues from different perspectives, I remain grateful that Peter was part of the youth group I organized and coordinated and deeply grateful for the way he continues what he began to do back then, i.e. to reflect upon significant religious questions and issues with great seriousness and deep regard for their importance. Were either of us running for public office, I am certain he would never vote for me and I am equally aware that I would not be voting for him.

Yet, from my perspective, the world of religion needs more of what I think we share, i.e. a willingness to see goodness in the other, even when our opinions clash with great regularity!

---

282 For the record, that is not exactly what I said! However, it is possible that I was not clear in my explanation. It is also possible that this person was quite intrigued and touched by the message of Fatima that became an integral part of his life of faith. Whatever the case may be, this interpretation definitely provides an example of how people leading such discussions need to be sure they explore in detail. Looking back many years, I would suggest that it is possible that I fell somewhat short of doing so. Having said that, I would nonetheless say that my perception of Fatima, as well as of other claims of apparitions, and this young person's were quite different.

283 These reviews are available on THE STREAM, a resource for many conservative Roman Catholics. Peter has served for several years as a conservative Catholic leader in Connecticut.

CLEAR, CONCISE, AND MEANINGFUL PREACHING

The presence of a message within the service of worship has been an integral part of organized Christianity since its very beginnings. In worship services within different Christian traditions, the sermon (called homily by some) is considered to have a unique importance to it.

Depending on the traditions of various churches, there is considerable variety regarding the length of this message. In addition, again, based on church practice, the sermon's place in the overall liturgy depends on several factors. Historically, in many Protestant churches, it has not been unusual to see something of a build up to the preaching of the sermon, with the sermon providing a starting point for people to go out and live out their week, until they return to next week's experience of worship.

In the liturgical traditions within Catholicism, Orthodox Christianity and several Protestant denominations, Word and Sacrament together form the core of worship. In my view, the Evangelical Lutheran Church in America has provided a wonderful outline of worship in its fourfold presentation of worship as involving the acts of Gathering, Hearing the Word, Sharing the Meal and then the final act of Sending, i.e., going out into the world and living out that which one affirms at worship.

Historically, especially in churches with full blown liturgy such as I describe above, the sermon had tended not to take on the centrality found in some other denominations. However, over the last several decades, the importance of homiletics, i.e., preaching, has found an emphasis in the worship life of the wide variety of Christian churches, even those which tended not to emphasize it previously.

The bottom line is this: Preaching is an important and integral part of worship.

One could go on at great length as to the why of this, something I choose not to do right here. However, I find it important to say this: A well prepared and delivered sermon opens the door to reflect on SOMETHING OF IMPORTANCE as expressed in the passage of Scripture around which the sermon (homily) is centered.

Consequently, the key to worthwhile worship is expressed in the three words I have stated above. Good preaching should be :

CLEAR — A preacher needs to be certain that, at some point, she/he makes the main point. One hopes that a person who hears the message can go away with a strong sense of what the preacher was saying!

CONCISE — A sermon should not be an extended academic lecture. The main question a preacher needs to ask her/himself is: *If I were sitting in the pew listening to this sermon, would I be able to summarize the essence of the message?*

MEANINGFUL — There should be a relevance to the message. Unfortunately, there are so many terrible things going on in this world that provide material for sermons. Without stretching things out, a preacher should find a way of connecting the words of Jesus and/or the various Biblical writers with something that is relevant to the congregation worshiping that day. Examples might include issues regarding the morality of war and conscientious objection, civil rights or such matters as the insurrection on the nation's Capital as supported by a good number of Christians, and issues raised by such horrific matters of the murders of George Floyd as well as the young man in Memphis just a few months prior to the publication of this book.

I would also add that it should be prepared with a recognition of the particular "audience" who will be hearing this message.

MUSIC THAT TOUCHES THE HEART AND MIND

I want to start here by making two observations:

1. In many churches, the selection of hymns is found in the one or two hymnals in peoples' pews.
2. In some churches, including some in which I have either served or done supply preaching, despite the presence of a hymn book or two in the pews, the congregation has become used to

singing a small number of hymns which are to be found within the hymnal. Many other pieces of music from the hymn book have never been experienced by the people in the pews. In fact, while I have been fortunate, thankfully, to have good relations with those I have served in congregations over the years, I nevertheless will get some legitimate, pushback style questions regarding why I have incorporated some hymns that have not been part of that congregation's worship life.

At various times, I have tried my best to explain what I consider to be the importance of providing an *antidote to the "We have always done things this way" that has all too often seeped into church worship.*

This leads us to:

3. *The importance of variety in church music!*

This requires a spirit of openness within a congregation which can be fostered by church leaders, including, though not limited to the pastor, who engage in communicating to their congregations about the important place of music in the worship life of the church. This could include a sermon occasionally in which the preacher explores the topic of music at worship.

In some churches in which I have served either as the church's pastor or a substitute supply preacher, I have discovered that the variety of music utilized is extremely limited. In reviewing the bulletins in some churches I have been in, it was clear to me both that a relatively small number of hymns were used over a long period of time AND that there were some hymns well known within Christian worship circles that were never sung in the particular church where I was either serving on a regular basis or providing supply.

At times, when I was organizing the service and suggested some specific music, I was even told that this suggestion of mine was for a hymn the congregation had never heard. I tried to ensure people that my response was polite as I noted to some folks that there is a wide body of music within the overall historic Christian traditions and that many hymns they have never heard were fairly easy to pick up upon.

A WAY TO APPROACH THIS

I see the following as helpful ways to approach these issues as well as the possible pushback from people who are concerned about good worship:

The pastor should:

1. Be conversant in church music and theology. He/she should keep up to date with trends in church music and have a strong working knowledge of a variety of church hymnals of varied denominations.
2. Be comfortable with presiding at blended worship services. *By this I mean services that may show some variation from time to time, including that found in different musical expressions!*
3. Keep up to date both with respect to theology and to church music by doing serious research on the hymnals of other denominations and the hymns and other music contained therein.
4. Focus on a consistent approach to how blended worship is done!

There is no way around the basic fact that a pastor whose role is to serve as a worship leader in her/his congregation needs to have a strong knowledge of the variety present in Christian hymnody and overall liturgy. The pastor, for the most part, is charged with the responsibility of preaching sermons and structuring the liturgy of the congregation. Consequently, she or he should be expected to have a good deal of knowledge. In addition. she/he should have a strong sense of the worship styles and options found in other denominations and the value (or lack thereof) of integrating these styles and options into the worship experience in her/his church congregation.

> *For the most part, this is not the knowledge about music that a good musician/music director would possess. Rather it is about what is SAID in the lyrics of each hymn and where those lyrics both fit in to the message being preached and the Scriptures being read and heard.*

Another important piece of knowledge that a pastor should have would be of the wide variety of hymnals and other church music resources currently available. It is quite likely that one may discover hymns that are in the hymn books of other denominations and not to be found in the hymnals in the pews of her/his church.

> *A church musician should have the ability to play a wide variety of hymns. It would be advisable, If possible, for that musician to have knowledge of a large number of them as well. In our contemporary church context, a church musician, even if she/he has a special interest in the old, traditional hymns, should be conversant in the wide variety of Christian music being published and recorded these days. The pastor should have that awareness as well.*
>
> *It is the responsibility of a pastor to evaluate whether some of the language contained within certain hymns is of questionable theological merit. In addition, a pastor needs to be very attentive to the use of inclusive language in hymnody and how to deal with hymns that are clearly male dominated in their language.*[284]

QUITE FORTUNATE

I have been most fortunate that in several churches I have served, I have done so alongside a musician whom I first met when I served at his church when he was 15.[285] I cite him here as an example of what I am saying in my comments above. In addition, I have mentioned him earlier in this book as well.

---

284 This is VERY important!
285 Eric R. Hutchinson, to whom I have referred earlier.

Eric Hutchinson is an extremely skilled musician with a degree from one of the finest music programs in the United States.[286] In addition to having grown up around church music, he was also active as a high school and a college student in providing the musical scores for some plays performed by adolescents and young adults at the church to which he belonged in his formative years.

Over the years, we have worked together in many churches. I cite Eric here as exemplary in that he has a strong feel for much of the traditional music that has been part of the services at which he has played keyboard over the course of many years as well as an outstanding working knowledge of a variety of church music, including some that may be found on contemporary Christian music labels. In addition, he is highly skilled in playing what some might call popular tunes that can be incorporated into worship services.

While he is not the traditional church organist, he brings a unique blend in both his keyboard ability and in leading the singing for the congregation, making them quite comfortable in joining in and singing along, along the way presenting them with unique, special church hymns for church use with which they had not been familiar before. I am grateful as well that over the years we have worked together, he has introduced me to some church hymns that I now count among my favorites!

In the way he leads the music in the congregations he has served, Eric makes a major contribution toward engaging the congregation in the worship experience through an approach to music that speaks deeply to one's heart, as opposed to a robotic approach all too often found in the worship experiences of a good number of congregations. It is quite clear that attracting a capable music director is a major plus in any congregation! I have been so fortunate to have had Eric serve with me in several congregations throughout.

---

286 Berklee College of Music, Boston, Massachusetts.

SPIRITUALITY IN AN ECUMENICAL AND INTERFAITH CONTEXT

In concluding this chapter, I propose for your consideration the following:

1. *I suggest that church leaders in mainline Protestant, as well as Catholic and Orthodox churches, go out of their way to connect with leaders in other congregations of differing backgrounds and denominations to find ways to share a variety of worship experiences together.*
2. *I recommend that wherever possible particular attention is given to shared events during specific seasons of the church calendar year.*

From my experience, one of the finest examples of this occurred when I served as a pastor in the city of Manchester, Connecticut.

For many years prior to the onset of the COVID-19 pandemic, the churches in this middle-sized city joined together for a walk through the center of town on Good Friday, with the walk being an opportunity to share in the devotions connected with the Way of the Cross. This event brought together Protestants and Catholics alike and was most likely joined as well by those without religious affiliation who sensed something rather significant within this experience.

As part of the walk, along the way folks would stop at several of the many churches for a time of prayer before moving on and continuing the walk.

A former youth group member of mine from my days in one of Manchester's Catholic parishes, someone whom I have mentioned earlier in this book, is an active writer and has posted quite regularly about church related issues. He is a conservative Catholic and a strong believer in the importance of his Catholic faith. [287]

While he and I differ on a variety of theological matters, I share with him the conviction that this shared celebration of the Way of the Cross on the streets of his hometown on Good Friday

---

287 Peter Wolfgang, referred to previously in this book.

was truly a meaningful experience and I echo his appeal that it be brought back. I would be pleased to attend it even now when I am no longer connected directly to a town in which I used to serve both as a teacher and a pastor.[288]

3. As I have said earlier in this book, I would advocate for the establishment of connections between and among churches who could share in ecumenical youth ministry on a fairly regular basis. While in some cases, there may be difficulties here, there are real possibilities as well.

I would also suggest that worship teams be formed in local congregations and that these teams would be charged with exploring a variety of worship options which could be shared with other congregations within that locale. This would include the use of worship forms and styles from each other's denominational background.

CONSIDER THE FOLLOWING:

I suggest both:

1. that opportunities be offered for lay leadership of specific worship services.
2. that people find ways to make peace with the fact that some services are not well attended. I am convinced that if word were to get out about the value of a particular service, the numbers would increase. Consequently, I would suggest working hard on doing the very best one can to offer meaningful worship!
3. I would also recommend that churches on the local level consider getting together to provide programming that includes reaching out to those in need.

---

288 I had served as Director of Religious Education at St. Bridget Roman Catholic Church in Manchester as well as Youth Group leader there. In addition, I had also worked coordinating Religious Education for middle and high school students at St. James Catholic Church, where I also served as their youth minister as well!

4. *In short, my sincere conviction is that it is SO crucial that churches work as best they can to expand the possibilities for meaningful spiritual life within their congregations and also to do so in association with others. As an outgrowth of this approach, members and friends of these congregations will find ways to engage in spirituality that is anything but rote and routine but instead quite relevant as they face the living out of their everyday lives.*

RETHINKING RELIGIOUS EDUCATION

Those of us who for some reason have familiarity with the institutional church know that "religious education programming" has long been an integral part of the structure found within congregations.

Depending upon the denomination, there are a variety of programs contained under the general umbrella of "religious education." As a rule, such programming is very focused on children in a good number of congregations. Those connected to Protestant denominations would tend to use the term "Sunday School" to describe one of the church's most important tasks. Roman Catholics tend to opt for the term "CCD", i.e. Confraternity of Christian Doctrine.

In mainline and Roman Catholic churches, a key part of religious education programming consists of preparing children and young adolescents to celebrate certain significant rituals in their lives as Christians. In many of these churches, children have been baptized either as infants or at a very young age. While infant baptism is most common and normative within many of these churches, there is also an understanding that parents may decide to have their children baptized at an older age. Oftentimes in my experience as a pastor, this has occurred at a point in the parents' life when, for some reason or another, they sense the importance of this experience of Baptism in the life of a child. Some connect it with the eventual possibility of preparing for and ultimately receiving Communion. Others see it as a way of reconnecting the family unit with the community of church. [289]

Many congregations, Catholic, Protestant and Orthodox alike, have established religious education programming within their churches which both offer preparation for these special events as well as providing children with information about the Bible, as well as the key beliefs of the church to which that family is connected.

Thus, it is common for many congregations to offer programming in religious education for both younger and older children which follows this pattern:

1. The church provides preschool programming.
2. Vacation Bible School is incorporated into the church calendar.
3. Youth are engaged in preparation for reception of Communion and, in the Roman Catholic tradition, the celebration of Reconciliation. In some churches, this would involve preparation for celebration of a believers' Baptism, as alluded to previously.[290]
4. Young people would participate in a program of preparation for Confirmation which would ordinarily take place at some point in early to middle adolescence.
5. Many churches would establish opportunities to participate in what has been commonly called a "Youth Group." This group is open both to those who are preparing for Confirmation or have already been confirmed. In some churches, youth group

---

289 It is important to note that the Baptist tradition includes an individual making a free decision to be baptized at an age in which she/he can understand its meaning. Other denominations offer baptism at an early age. A good number of parents have had their infant and young children baptized in the churches with which these parents have been connected. Note: In many churches, pastors have opted to baptize children of parents who are not members or active participants in those churches. Over the course of my own pastorates, I have been very comfortable with making that my approach.
290 This refers to Baptisms in which the person being baptized is aware of and adheres to the Baptismal commitment.

participation is mandated as a required step toward being confirmed.

IMPORTANT NOTE:

There is some degree of variety present in the religious educational programming found in churches. What I have described above is a general overview.

A GRADUATION MINDSET

What is quite common in the religious programming found in many churches is something I would call a *"graduation mindset"* which is to be found in both young people and their parents (and grandparents) alike. By this, I mean that many adults see their responsibility as providing the opportunity for their children to learn about religion and their faith. They believe that it is important to have their children participate in classes held within their church. They also take the position that after their daughters or sons have gone through the church's process and have "graduated" [291], the parents have done their job and their children need not be required to attend such classes any longer.

Try as they might to find ways to "hold on" to their youth, in many congregations there will be an inevitable drop off in youth participation both in worship and in other church programs as soon as they finish up the necessary requirements for Confirmation or, in some churches, believers' Baptism." [292]

THE SUBSEQUENT REALITY

The bottom line in all of this is that many young people lose their connection with the church once they have gone through all the required

---

291 A popular phrase for completing one's formal Religious Education experience
292 Baptist churches

hoops. Parents understandably take comfort in the fact that they have done their jobs.

MY CONCERN

It is extremely important to me that I make clear that my intention is NOT to be critical of these parents. TO THE CONTRARY, my concern is with how many churches, without intention, have set up a system that is really based on a graduation mentality. I have heard parents tell their children who are less than thrilled with having to participate in these programs that they just have to keep putting up with CCD or Sunday School or Confirmation classes for just a little longer!

HOVERING OVER ALL OF THIS...

With the exception to be found in some very active congregations, the reality exists that what adolescents find themselves seeing in their local congregations are these simple facts:

1. Many of their own parents do not attend worship with any regularity.
2. While some youth DO have parents who help with church events and activities, for most adults in congregations, religious education stopped when they finished off their own requirements as adolescents. In some cases, these parents may very well have been pretty much finished with church back when they completed the requirements found in their churches when they were young themselves.
3. Even more concerning is the reality that while many parents make a point of attending worship as needed during the time their children are engaged in preparation, this tends to fade once their daughters and sons have gone through all of the necessary steps.

PLEASE READ THIS CAREFULLY...

All the available data indicates that the parents of today's adolescents grew up in a time when a lot of changes were occurring in the churches to which they may have been connected. Assuming that many of the young people who are attending Sunday School, Baptism or Confirmation classes, have parents who are in the age range of their 30's to 40's, I would contend that the relationship of parents to church is quite different from earlier days, including those days many years ago when I was growing up

A STARTING POINT

One of the greatest concerns expressed by the leadership of many churches is that there really are not a lot of children and youth around. The reason for this is obvious: *The membership and attendance patterns of many churches tend to favor senior citizens.* In these recent years in which the pandemic was front and center, many churches offered online worship services for those who preferred to stay at home. In grazing through the internet and tuning in on some of those services, it was amazing how the number of us gray haired older folks stood out!

As I have stated earlier, my experience has been that in mainline congregations, a high number of attendees would fall in the category of "senior citizens". Consequently, there are not as many young people as desired to participate in educational programs such as Sunday School, Confirmation preparation, and Youth Group. *This should never grant an easy pass to a church to just give up on programming for those in these age groupings.*

I would contend that this could quite readily be countered in the following ways:

1. Churches need to find a way to offer an educational program to children of *all ages* which would be held in the church building or possibly the homes of those willing to volunteer.

2. In addition, they should look for ways to connect with other local mainline churches on occasion.

> *What I am saying is that the church should make clear both to people who are participants in it as well as to those in the local community outside of its walls that, simply put, THEY WILL OFFER PROGRAMS FOR CHILDREN AND OLDER YOUTH. The fact that "We don't have enough kids" should not be seen as an excuse! Nor should "We tried some adult education programs in our church, but it did not work."*

The same willingness to reach out to other mainline churches in the neighborhood is something that should be evident in developing youth ministry in local communities.

DIFFERENT APPROACHES TO THIS:

A SHARED EVENT LEADING TO SHARED OUTREACH

> *It is most likely more important than ever that mainline churches within cities and towns find ways to offer programs together.* This is NOT to take away from what they offer their own congregants. However, it can be a very expansive way of offering a variety of worship services as well as opportunities for outreach to congregations engaged in working together!

I am convinced that wonderful things can happen when churches pool their resources to offer a variety of programming, much of which can be directed to offering opportunities for people to support important causes which churches should support.

Inviting Local Youth Groups To Your Church

One of my best memories from my days serving as a youth minister came when I held that position in one of the Roman Catholic churches in Manchester, Connecticut. What deems it so memorable is that with such superb young people who were excited about and committed to youth ministry, along with some outstanding adult volunteers who saw the importance of it as well, we were able to host an ecumenical youth ministry event at which young people who were active in local Protestant churches were invited to participate.

remember the excitement I felt witnessing young people gathering to discuss topics of importance along with just simply spending time enjoying being in each other's company.

> *From my most recent experiences in churches, these ec-umenical activities have simply not been happening. To me, that is a significant loss for young people as well as those adults who seek to help create the space for youth partici-pation.*

Encouraging Invites From Other Churches

If clergy from local congregations as well as lay persons in various positions, e.g. Director of Religious or Christian Education, establish relationships with other churches, the possibilities for future collaboration grow and when they occur, they most likely be perceived as quite worthwhile!

An Openness To Those Churches That May Have Different Theological Perspectives

This brings along a key question: What about conservative Christian churches? Is a youth group experience involving conservative evangelical churches, Catholics, and mainline Protestant churches even a possibility?

It is here that I wish to share an example from my days as Youth Group leader in a Roman Catholic parish, several years before I left the Catholic Church:

When I was serving as this group's leader, I sought to, on occasion, invite the youth groups of local non-Catholic churches to be part of one of our Youth Group evenings. In one of those events, the approach to the Bible expressed by the other church's youth differed from how the Bible was understood within the Catholic community.[293] Some of the differences were quite apparent. However, because of the openness and kindness of both the adults and teens from that other church, we were able to engage in a very positive evening which culminated in a meaningful concluding time of prayer and song!

It is important to do this whenever possible. In some cases, it simply cannot happen. It would be in those situations where particular participants see their theological or Biblical perspective as containing "absolute truth." [294] This kind of locked in position makes dialogue difficult and often impossible.

It is also important that church youth be given opportunities to engage in interfaith learning. It was not that long ago when a common practice in Youth Groups both Catholic and Protestant was a visit by young people in Christian churches to a Jewish synagogue in their community. During that visit, it was typical that the local Rabbi would speak to the students about Judaism, its rituals, and its history.

My experience has been that what was once a trend has faded into the background. Much of this is attributable to the onset of COVID, of course, but there is much more to it than that. *It speaks of a diminished reality within churches to find ways to connect with those beyond its walls.* The subsequent result is diminished oppor-

---

293 This church belonged to the Christian Reformed Church denomination.
294 This as opposed to a relativism that many conservative Christians see as problematic!

tunities for young people to explore the possibilities of spirituality within the broader religious context within their world.

More than ever, what was typical in the exciting interfaith days from the 1960's is needed in this, our own place and time. In my view, young people (and adults as well) should be offered the opportunities to learn more about various religious traditions.

As a pastor within the Protestant tradition, I would strongly advocate for educational opportunities for youth and adults alike that point young people and adults toward a deeper understanding of religious traditions such as Buddhism, Hinduism, Islam, the Quaker experience and more, including Roman Catholicism and Orthodox faith.

As I see it, this is a necessary part of an approach to religious education which is more than a routine and rote experience. Instead, it is one that provides those participating with the opportunity to examine the depth of religious experience as perceived by people from varied traditions. These experiences provide insights for those participating that help them see the universality of the religious experience and the points of connection between and among them.

A VERY IMPORTANT QUESTION: WHAT ABOUT MAINLINE PROTESTANT – CATHOLIC INTERACTION?

In addressing the question of whether Protestant and Catholic churches should take more opportunities to both worship and share educational programming together, in addition to forging social ties which would naturally lead to shared outreach to those in need, we need to recognize a very important fact:

> *As a result of the explosion in ecumenism, i.e. the shared relationship between Protestants and Catholics, the late 1960's and early 1970's were filled with opportunities for Catholics and Protestants to pray together, share in common worship, learn from the worship practices of the other, advocate for important social causes, and draw closer to understanding and living out the bonds of Christian unity.*

*THAT IS NO LONGER THE CASE! While the Second
Vatican Council had a great impact on Catholicism and its
practices, much of what the Council espoused is not put into
practice within much of contemporary Catholicism.*

Back then, which was really not that many years ago, there
was great vitality within Catholic seminaries that trained priests
and within Catholic colleges and universities that offered exciting
academic programs for those who were not ordained but sought
to live out active ministry in the church.

What happened at Vatican II and the development of significant Catholic theological writing pointed to the possibilities
of significant shared ecumenical commitment between mainline
Protestant churches and Roman Catholics.

In my view, some of the finest theological writing could be
found in the work of the distinguished theologian Richard P. Mc-
Brien. McBrien was a priest in the Archdiocese of Hartford who
headed the Institute for Religious Education at Boston College,
which I attended, and then became chair of the Department of
Theology at the University of Notre Dame.

When I attended graduate school at Boston College, I was
still a Roman Catholic and my experience as a student there was
very exciting. In my program there, I was given the opportunity
to interact with distinguished theological scholars. The classes I
attended as I pursued this degree included those taught by highly
renowned Catholic scholars, including McBrien, Richard McCormick, S.J, Anthony Padovano, Gloria Durka, Gabriel Moran and
many others. The distinguished writer and poet James Carroll,[295]
a former Paulist priest, also participated in programs at Boston
College's institute and offered opportunities for students there to
have thought provoking interactions!

Students in this graduate program took their learning and
established careers in the fields of Roman Catholic Religious Edu-

---

295 An incredible writer. I recommend his books highly! I have found them
    to be incredibly inspirational.

cation as did I when I assumed a position overseeing Catholic Youth Ministry in the Diocese of Providence, Rhode Island. Students took leadership positions as teachers in Catholic high schools and colleges, members of diocesan staffs overseeing programs related to social justice, ecumenism, and current trends in Catholic theology.

At that time, as noted earlier in this book, many jobs were available to graduates of these programs and many ordained priests and religious women [296] whom I knew also took advantage of the growth opportunities to be found through participating in these educational opportunities.

BUT THEN SOMETHING HAPPENED...

What you are about to read contains opinions that are quite critical of the changes that have occurred within Roman Catholicism. With that in mind, it is extremely important that I make things quite clear. I have expounded at length about some of these opinions in some of my other writings.[297] While I do not want to be redundant and hope that I am not, it is important that the reader of this book is offered a clear understanding of where the positions I have taken come. I will try to be as concise as possible:

VATICAN II

- One of the most important and significant events in the Roman Catholic Church was the Second Vatican Council (1962-65).
- One could go on in depth giving a history of the background that led to this Council.
- Suffice it to say, its results led to significant changes in the Catholic Church and perhaps even more importantly, provided great hope that changes were about to come.

---

296 Many religious sisters were graduate school students in this program at Boston College.
297 I have referred to these throughout this book.

This Council, about which much has been written, was supported and endorsed by Pope John XXIII. Following his death, his successor Pope Paul VI took up the work of the Council and in his own way, embraced its spirit.

- The result led to specific documents being developed that would lead local dioceses throughout the world to explore a variety of changes within their local churches.
- As a result of the Council:
- Latin was no longer the required language of worship. Congregations began to pray in their vernacular language.
- The role of the lay person was given high priority. There was a shift toward a recognition of the importance of lay leadership within the church.
- There was an explosion of theological writings that became part of the educational programs in Catholic colleges and universities. Students and seminarians began reading author/theologians such as Karl Rahner, Teilhard de Chardin [298], Hans Kung, Richard McCormick, Charles Curran and more. I have referred to some of these names throughout this book.
- *In what might arguably be the most significant move in terms of overall perception of changes in the church, the altar was turned around and now the priest would face the people.* This liturgical renewal also had an impact on many churches in the Protestant tradition and CANNOT BE UNDERESTIMATED! While it may have seemed to some like a minor move, it came with significant theological implications. This communicated a connection between the presider at the Communion table and those within the congregation. In a real sense, the congregation could readily perceive itself as gathered at a table, as opposed to the witness of what could be experienced as a far away action.

---

298 During my years at Holy Cross, I benefited from reading and discussing the writings of Pierre Teilhard de Chardin, S. J., as taught by Rev. Paul Harmon, a wonderful Jesuit priest and scholar. Sadly, my experience has been that some of the finest Catholic theologians have either been critiqued unfairly or outright ignored by those on the Catholic Right!

What is most significant here for Christians, of course, is the presence of Jesus right there at table, not a faraway God, but rather present in our very midst. One could readily think here of Bonhoeffer's expression of "the beyond in our midst". [299]

• Religious education picked up incredible vitality. Annual Conferences for professional church educators and lay persons who taught CCD and worked with youth exploded in numbers.

These events sponsored by Catholic dioceses both drew huge crowds and brought in tremendous speakers. I will never forget the New England Congress of Religious Education event I attended on the campus of the University of New Hampshire sometime after Vatican II. The crowd was huge, and the speakers included some of the finest theologians, religious education professionals and liturgists within the Catholic Church in this country. A few years later, I attended a similar one in Springfield, Massachusetts. Simply being an attendee at these and many more I had the opportunity to attend was a privilege for which I will always be grateful. At that time and for many years later, I was also invited to speak at a good number of youth related events within Catholic parishes and other settings where large numbers of religious educators, youth and those who worked with them were present.[300] That was really a wonderful experience!

After I completed my Master's degree in Religious Education, I had the opportunity to work as a coordinator of Youth Ministry in the office of a Roman Catholic diocese.[301] I remember those days as ones filled with great vitality in the variety of programs accessible to Catholic youth. In addition, I was impressed with the level of interest regarding the implementation of Vatican II that was present

---

299 This is an important theological point! Please give it some serious thought!!!
300 This included at many local churches and in a variety of programs outside of my home state.
301 Diocese of Providence, Rhode Island.

in so many of the priests, sisters and lay persons whom I had come to know during that time.

THE PONTIFICATE OF JOHN PAUL II

What you are about to read contains an honest expression of many of my concerns about what happened to Catholicism during the pontificates of Pope John Paul II and his successor Pope Benedict.

Karol Wojtyla was chosen to be Pope in 1978 and took the name Pope John Paul II.[302] His pontificate ended with his death in 2005. From 1978-1999, I remained an active participant in the Roman Catholic Church. During these twenty-one years of his pontificate, I worked in the Catholic Church as a Permanent Deacon, Director of Religious Education, and religion teacher in a Roman Catholic high school.[303] When this Pope came to Boston and spoke to a huge crowd on the Boston Common, I stood in the rain for hours along with a Catholic friend who continues to serve as an ordained Permanent Deacon in order to have the opportunity to hear the Pope speak. I had never been this close to a Pope in my entire Roman Catholic life!

YEARS LATER...

In 1998, during the pontificate of John Paul II, I made the difficult decision to leave the Roman Catholic Church. This decision ultimately led to my eventual ordination in the ministry of the United Church of Christ.[304]

SOME IMPORTANT FACTS

Pope John Paul II was a theological scholar and was also a highly respected leader of the Catholic Church in Poland. He is to be commended for his dedication to a people who had undergone considerable oppression for all too many years.

---

302 It is customary for Popes to take a name when elected to the papacy.
303 As noted throughout this book
304 March 3, 2002

One would have to label Polish Roman Catholicism as quite traditional and conservative. The pontificate of John Paul II and that of Pope Benedict, a German bishop who would follow him, had an impact upon Roman Catholicism in several different and significant ways:

- There were major changes in the materials published within the Catholic Church for use in parish religious education. In addition, a trend developed whereby local Catholic diocesan newspapers held back from presenting differing viewpoints on a variety of issues and focused instead on affirming the official teaching of the church on these matters.

- This approach was quite noteworthy in what was my home diocese during my time as an adult within the Catholic Church. While for many years, with the approval of Archbishop Whealon, the diocesan newspaper *The Catholic Transcript* carried a weekly column by Father Richard McBrien, this column was eliminated at a time when a rather conservative priest had become the bishop of that archdiocese.[305] This trend has continued even to this day as the now monthly, as opposed to weekly, publication, for all intents and purposes, offers articles and pictures that , in my view, are heavily reflective of a pre Vatican II mindset.

- In reading these publications, I am reminded of documents I once saw in some of the classrooms I was in during my early Catholic school days in very traditionally Catholic Putnam, Connecticut.

- Catholic religious education as taught in parishes changed considerably.

- Catholic liturgy underwent changes which included the return of pre-Vatican II prayers and responses in the liturgy of the church.

- It became typical for diocesan bishops to send potential seminarians to very conservative seminaries. Excellent

seminaries which had trained many priests throughout the
years ceased to be places of learning for a good number of
potential priests.

• Catholic bookstores, which used to be quite active in the light
of Vatican II, resorted to a new approach as they eliminated
books which raised questions and challenged much of
conservative Catholic teaching. Some very good ones also
closed. [306]

• Over the course of time, the door began closing on the
possibility of ordaining women to the priesthood. Even in the
heyday of this movement, it was nonetheless quite tenuous.
Organizations within the church that advocated for married
clergy, women priests and deacons and other steps toward
renewal, while in most cases still existing, had lost their
intensity and passion.[307]

• In the United States and elsewhere, the church experienced
the profound effects of the priest sex abuse crisis.

As time moved on, the church experienced:

• *A conservative trend in the selection of those who were preparing
for the Permanent Diaconate. From my own experience, that
traditionalist Catholic approach was quite present among those
who trained for this ministry.*

• *A decline in candidates for the priesthood coupled with a closing
of many seminaries which included*

• *significant changes in the seminaries to which candidates for the
priesthood were assigned by their Bishop.*

• *A decline in church attendance*

• *The emergence of traditionalist clergy throughout the church in
significant contrast to the trends that were part of the time period
of excellent, more progressive clergy! This traditionalism included
a return to varied devotions and vestments that were part of*

---

306 This included one not far from my home in Connecticut and located in
the heart of Hartford, Connecticut.

307 This is in comparison to the busy days following Vatican II!

Catholicism from before Vatican II, the experience of Catholicism that I had in my early days at St. Mary's and at the Provincial House. [308]

• *Significant changes in worship. This included a return to forms of worship that were used prior to the Second Vatican Council.* [309]

THE EXPERIENCE OF FRANCIS

As I have written elsewhere, I believe the Catholic Church was extremely fortunate in the election of Pope Francis. In so many ways, he has presented a positive image of the Roman Catholic Church. Having said that, the fact remains that much of what had been established during the pontificates of Pope John Paul as well as his successor Pope Benedict has remained in place during the time when Francis has served as Pope. An example of this is the changes found in the celebration of the liturgy, as I have described above.

SEEKING COMMON SHARING WITH CATHOLIC CHURCHES

Despite all the impediments that have been built up over the years, it is my conviction that pastors of mainline Protestant churches need to both develop good interaction with Catholic clergy in their areas and work toward seeking out opportunities for:

- *Shared youth group discussions and activities*
- *Ecumenical prayer experiences*
- *Shared adult education presentations and dialogue*

---

308 I described this earlier in this book!

309 This is seen in the current text for the celebration of Mass in the Roman Catholic Church. What concerns me is that Pope Francis has not taken strong enough action to recapture the spirit of Vatican II by supporting significant changes in the celebration of liturgy. See my comments below for more on my thoughts about a wonderful man, Pope Francis!

ADULT EDUCATION PROGRAMMING

Having said this, it is also important to acknowledge that many mainline churches, for all intents and purposes, have given up on good Adult Education programming. With the many responsibilities that clergypersons have, coupled with the fact that a good number are serving in a part time capacity [310], it is a fact that it is quite easy to be overwhelmed with the responsibilities one has as a pastor.

HOWEVER, I wish to stress the tremendous IMPORTANCE of providing such opportunities. Even if initial attempts at adult religious education yield very few participants, my point of emphasis here is simple:

DO NOT GIVE UP!

As I see it, mainline churches offer the possibility of presenting those connected to them with a working knowledge of written materials that represent a depth in understanding the many complex questions to be found within the Christian tradition.

Unfortunately, the opportunity to explore these issues is extremely limited within congregations and among the public which frequents bookstores. With some exceptions, in the Religion section of many of these stores, you will find a preponderance of materials by very conservative writers, many of whom come from Protestant megachurches. You will also find very few publications from more progressive Catholic authors. I view this as extremely problematic and would contend that it is the role of mainline churches to help point people in the direction of other worthwhile theological resources.

---

310 This includes oftentimes sharing time with more than one church. Please see my book *Part Time Pastor, Full Time Church, Pilgrim Press.*

A SUGGESTED STARTING POINT FOR PROTESTANT CONGREGATIONS (AND ROMAN CATHOLIC AND ORTHODOX AS WELL):

- I would encourage local church communities to invite those from other churches and the wider community to Adult Education and Youth programming in their churches.
- I would also encourage ecumenical youth activity as I have described earlier in this book.
- Most importantly, even where there are differences, DO NOT GIVE UP on opportunities to engage in healthy ecumenical dialogue and to form good relationships!
- AND - DO NOT WORRY if initial turnouts are small. It is nonetheless a meaningful way to plant some very important seeds!

CLERGY SHOULD NOT GIVE UP

The support and presence of clergy within the churches is extremely important. In addition to spending time intermingling with people in their congregations and those in a broader ecumenical setting, because of their training and continuing education, they can be valuable resources for book studies on a variety of important topics.[311]

Again- SO WHAT IF THERE ARE SMALL NUMBERS IN ATTENDANCE? It is nonetheless an important starting point!

WHAT CATHOLICS AND PROTESTANTS CAN DO TOGETHER — PRAY ...

Even with the rise in the number of conservative and traditionalist Catholic churches, I believe that Protestant clergy leaders and

---

311 As an outgrowth of their graduate training in theology and responsibilities to keep up with current thinking, these clergy can serve as great resources!

lay leaders in their congregations should work hard to offer shared prayer experiences with Roman Catholic and Orthodox Christians.

There are several possible ways to do this:

- Consider sharing in Holden Evening Prayer [312], especially during the Lenten season.
- Offer Adult Education presentations from clergy of different traditions leading to dialogue regarding the different theological positions found in different churches.
- Offer services from the prayer books of other Christian churches. Perhaps Catholics and Protestants alike could join in shared services from the Episcopal Book of Common Prayer.
- Consider a shared Protestant/ Catholic Stations of the Cross during the Lenten season.
- Find ways to share educational programs as well as social outreach in seasons of Advent and Lent.

SO WHAT IF THE NUMBERS ARE SMALL? THE SIMPLE ACT OF DOING THESE THINGS SPEAKS VOLUMES IN AND OF ITSELF

While initial efforts MAY YIELD small numbers, my sense is that those who attend will appreciate the opportunity AND my firm belief is that if a church becomes known for certain programs, over time, people WILL COME!

Word will get out! It is worth the perseverance it entails!

DON'T GIVE UP! DON'T EVER GIVE UP!

I will be honest: Over these past few years, as you have observed in reading this book, I have been quite troubled by the mainline church closures around me. No sooner had we moved into our new home a few years back when a local Episcopal Church closed. When driving one day through a section of a local town

---

312 A beautiful worship service. This is a simple service which is focused on the Evening Prayer tradition found in several denominations. The music for this service is that written by the composer Marty Haugen.

in Connecticut, I discovered the closure of a historic Methodist church as well. When turning the corner in the town in which we used to live one afternoon, I found out that a once active American Baptist church at which I had spoken years prior at the request of a coworker who was very active there, had given up their presence in this community. This is just a short list of some of what I've experienced that I find quite troubling!

This, for me, is exacerbated by the reality that as I drive through the many towns which surround me, I find an increasing plethora of churches that stress a literal, fundamentalist understanding of the Bible, which for many congregants often morphs into active participation in and support of political campaigns which are antithetical to the teachings of the Gospel. While this is quite commonplace in the South, it has permeated the so-called liberal East Coast as well.

THE NEED TO READ

A final important point I need to emphasize is that local churches need to offer opportunities for their congregants to keep up with some good, valuable opportunities to read good books and articles.

Here are some ways in which this can be done:

- Offer regular programs for adults and adolescents in which good materials relevant to the subject matter are available and used. An example would be that if one were offering a class on the Gospels, one would provide the participants selections from academic materials on the subject. There are some excellent online programs available. In addition, clergy can be very helpful in constructing educational sessions on these important topics.[313]

- Offer a variety of programs and engage people in suggesting topics they would like to see explored. Sadly, I have seen an unfortunate decline in these kinds of programs in many churches. Over the course of my time serving as a pastor, I have

---

313 This is an important role for clergy within congregations!

had experiences where I needed to establish adult educational programming that had not been a regular part of that church's routine. As I noted before, it was the Sundays I spent as a college student in a Lutheran church in Worcester, Mass and the leadership of that pastor that convinced me of the significance and importance of Adult Religious Education.[314]

- Consider doing these programs ecumenically wherever possible. Wouldn't it be great, for example, to have a Bible Study on the Gospel of Matthew whose participants included members and friends from several churches in the area? What would make this even better is if somehow, in hearing about these programs, the interested "unchurched" and those others simply interested in learning would participate!

- Having a well-stocked book section within the church building and allotting some budget money for the purchase of books. With this being done, it is important that the church then proceed to advertise its book area on its website, Facebook page, Twitter feed, in local media, as well as in its worship bulletin. In a church where reading Biblical and theological materials has not been commonplace, this is something that takes a great deal of work! However, it is worth it and quite necessary!

- Set money aside for the purchase of books that can be circulated within the congregation or might have enough appeal for people to go out and purchase them. In doing all of this, one is encouraging growth in faith through the dual dynamic of internalizing some reading which poses relevant questions and also providing worthwhile material for meaningful conversations.

- *Finally, it is important that these books are not repetitive, robotic, and simplistic.* Unfortunately, much "religious" material is. What is needed is a sharing of ideas in conversation about materials that may lead readers to pose all kinds of questions

---

314 Emanuel Lutheran Church, Worcester, Massachusetts.

and even to struggle. Churches do NOT need a "dumbing down" of important material!

The wrestling and the tensions that may arise from shared learning and dialogue among those from different religious perspectives are NOT bad things at all.

They even have a Biblical precedent with which we will now conclude this chapter:

From Genesis [315]

> ²² *That night Jacob got up and took his two wives, his two female servants and his eleven sons and crossed the ford of the Jabbok.* ²³ *After he had sent them across the stream, he sent over all his possessions.* ²⁴ *So Jacob was left alone, and a man wrestled with him till daybreak.* ²⁵ *When the man saw that he could not overpower him, he touched the socket of Jacob's hip so that his hip was wrenched as he wrestled with the man.* ²⁶ *Then the man said, "Let me go, for it is daybreak."*
>
> *But Jacob replied, "I will not let you go unless you bless me."*
>
> ²⁷ *The man asked him, "What is your name?"*
>
> *"Jacob," he answered.*
>
> ²⁸ *Then the man said, "Your name will no longer be Jacob, but Israel, because you have struggled with God and with humans and have overcome."*
>
> ²⁹ *Jacob said, "Please tell me your name."*
>
> *But he replied, "Why do you ask my name?" Then he blessed him there.*
>
> ³⁰ *So Jacob called the place Peniel, saying, "It is because I saw God face to face, and yet my life was spared."*
>
> ³¹ *The sun rose above him as he passed Peniel, and he was limping because of his hip.*

I love this passage - and HERE IS WHY:

The very process of engaging in religious education, including immersion in serious Bible Study, must be centered in a comfort level with asking questions. Much of what is found in Biblical writing is challenging and thought provoking.

---

315 Genesis 32:22-32.

Consequently, it is SO IMPORTANT that through meaningful religious education in the local church, people are given the opportunity and the freedom to really wrestle with what they have been hearing and reading. It is in that wrestling made possible by the simple presence of opportunities to READ and TO HEAR as well as TO DISCUSS...

It is in that wrestling that people can connect with that which gives meaning, purpose, significance and depth to our religious experience and thus to our very lives!

WE NEED TO RETHINK RELIGIOUS EDUCATION!

10

SO ... IS ANYBODY THERE? DOES ANYBODY CARE?

For one reason or another, religion has always been important to me. In reading that, please DO NOT put me on a pedestal. There is no way I would ever classify myself as "holier than thou."[316] That is for sure. In fact, a long time ago, I was struck by the insights of Martin Luther who was speaking both of himself and all of humanity when he identified himself as "*Simul Justus et Peccator*", translated simply as "*At the same time, justified and sinner.*" Those words of Luther made so much sense to me. This recognition that we human beings are capable of "falling short of the glory of God" [317] was something I came to embrace at a rather young age.

Having said that, I also have to say that the world of organized religion was one that was and to this day is still an important part of my life. Though I approach it as important, I also do not assert that it places me or anyone else moved in its direction as someone who would be "holier than thou". The French phrase *au contraire* [318] strikes me as a realistic description!

However, having honestly said all of that, sometimes I do find myself thinking that after spending so many years of my life in something I consider to be highly important, I am nonetheless left with this lingering question, articulated in a song I once heard,

---

316 A pejorative term, for sure!
317 Romans 3:23.
318 "To the contrary"

its title being rather plaintive and challenging indeed: *"Is Anybody There? Does Anybody Care?"*[319]

As the years have gone by, I have become more and more aware of how I have been so deeply immersed in, for want of a better term, the world of religion. In that world, I have really enjoyed having the opportunity to do a lot of interesting reading and to engage in leading worship, preaching, teaching, learning, and doing outreach to others in need. In so many ways, I have enjoyed being connected to church ministry, both in the time I was serving as an ordained Catholic clergyperson (Permanent Deacon) as well as in the ordained ministry of the United Church of Christ, with opportunities to serve in Evangelical Lutheran Church of America congregations and in other churches as well.[320]

As a matter of fact, I have found myself caring enough to have a deep concern as to how the very term RELIGION is perceived by those for whom church is either in their past or was never a real part of their lives.

To be honest, I have become quite troubled when I have heard people refer to "religion" as being connected solely with conservative Roman Catholicism and right-wing Evangelical Protestant Christianity. As much as I enjoy watching football, and I do, I find the simplistic expressions of faith found among evangelically based athletes to be quite troubling. It bothers me that Major League baseball has turned to an organization called Baseball Chapel, an evangelically based organization, to meet the spiritual needs of its athletes.[321]

While these approaches to religion represent expressions of Christianity, they lack the background and depth to be found in a more balanced and thorough approach to Christian faith.

Though I will concede that I may very well be coming across as quite critical, I would also contend that these issues surround-

---

319 From the play 1776
320 As described throughout this book!
321 This is a program which operates from an approach to Christianity that is evangelical and conservative.

ing what constitutes Christian faith are extremely important. The fact remains that there are clear cut differences under the broad umbrella of Christianity. As we have seen in the world of politics, some of these approaches are extremely troubling and do not reflect the essence of Christian faith. Over these last few years, we have seen this in the marriage of political "conservatism" [322] and religion.

A LIFE JOURNEY WITH PURPOSE

Over the course of my now rather long life, Christian faith, for better or worse, has been extremely important to me! I was, as you well know from reading this, exposed to it rather thoroughly when I was quite young and while I DID go through periods in my post college years where I was not attending Sunday worship with my usual regularity, the regularity that began when I was about 4 years old, my lack of attendance at worship during that time frame was rather short lived and worship has remained VERY important to me throughout my adult life!

AND...

Even during that period when I was rebelling against what I was experiencing within my native Roman Catholicism, the core of this rebellion was centered on my high expectations for what the church should and could be but was not.

---

322 In fairness, political conservatism has not always had the look found in the right wing extremism of many current politicians and their supporters. In the past, conservatism has not been associated with some of the extreme tendencies we have witnessed throughout these past few years! However, one could say that even when not overt, it has been simmering under the surface for several years, most notably found in some of the conservatism in some Republican factions several election cycles back.

CURRENT REALITY

What I have come to recognize, through my work in a variety of jobs outside of the church [323] and through the relationships I have formed over the years with friends and family members, is that there has been a rather steep decline in how organized religion has developed here in the United States since the 1960's and early 70's, those time periods in which I was transitioning into late adolescence and moving toward young adulthood.

BACKWARDS IN TIME

To express this reality more thoroughly, it is important that I have looked back on my childhood in my hometown of Putnam, Connecticut. While I have explained this thoroughly in some of my other writings [324], I nonetheless want to state some important facts that will be helpful to those who have not read those writings and will nonetheless still be relevant to those of you who have.

Simply put, in the hometown in which I grew up, Catholicism was alive, well and active. The Catholic school I attended was packed with hundreds of students, many girls who graduated from my school proceeded to go to an all-girls Catholic high school in town [325], a good number of guys went to a Catholic all male prep school a town over, as did I.

The town, as you have seen in your reading of this book, was home to the national headquarters of a community of sisters known as the Daughters of the Holy Spirit. As I have mentioned in my writing, I served them as their altar boy for over a decade in my young life. Suffice it to say, this town, including the large cemetery in which so many were buried, was immersed in its Catholic identity.[326]

---

323 My years in public education!

324 As I have noted throughout this book.

325 Putnam Catholic Academy

326 I notice this whenever I am back in Putnam and paying visit to my parents' graves. Inevitably, my experience there brings me back to so much of what you have read in the pages of this book!

CHANGING TIMES

The core of what I am saying is this:

My hometown was one in which a very large number of its residents were involved with St. Mary's Church and School. Mass attendance was high in this Catholic parish and pews tended to be quite full each Sunday morning. This was quite typical even on the days when it was snowing and people had to walk to church through the snow. I have fond memories of those days indeed!

Though I no longer live there and cannot say I have exceptionally close connections with those with whom I grew up, I can point out the fact that much like many Catholic parishes throughout our country, the number of people who attend Mass at my former home parish has dropped considerably. What once was a thriving weekend at St. Mary's is now comparatively very quiet. I have perused the Internet and have seen the information about the number of priests who serve there as well as the limited number of Masses offered as those priests are now required to go off to other churches and preside at Masses there! This is a far cry from the flurry of Sunday activity to be found back when I was young when we would follow up Sunday Mass with a side trip to Henry's Corner Store where folks would flock to get their morning paper [327] and to enjoy a delicious cup of coffee as well!

In addition, as you know from reading about the new private school in town, that Catholic high school for young women has been long gone and replaced. In fact, it has become rather well known nationally for its basketball program. That school has now taken over the Provincial House and the national headquarters of those wonderful nuns now operates with offices in a rather small building over the town line.

That truly outstanding Catholic elementary school which I attended, the one with an amazing reputation throughout New

---

327 For me , the Boston Globe, especially its sports section which covered all of my favorite professional teams!

England for youth football[328] and where I had served as a coach for basketball and baseball teams that did really well [329], has now been closed for years and it a distant part of Putnam's past as is the convent which housed the sisters who made so great a difference in my youth, a convent to which my Dad would often take groceries for the nuns and be sure that I came along to help him do so as well.[330]

SUNDAYS IN OUR TIME …

Nowadays, the Sundays of my youth have pretty much gone by. There are exceptions. In the South, I understand, especially in evangelical churches, a good number of children might show up for Sunday School and youth group too, often later on in their busy week. I see those exceptions even in New England as I drive by churches which one could label as evangelical, fundamentalist or at least conservative. [331] Yet, in most places that I know of where both Catholicism and Protestantism was quite active come Sunday mornings, the current scene is quite different.

In these modern days of ours, Sundays might be for playing golf, watching one's children play basketball, baseball, football, soccer or hockey, sitting in front of the TV, going to the park, beach or lake or participating in any number of activities of unique interest to those who reside there. For many, it is also a day to do some necessary shopping!

Attendance at Mass or at traditional Protestant services is down for the most part. I have seen this in my experience in both Catholic and Protestant churches and I have observed it in the data as well!

---

328 The St. Mary's football team, developed at coached by the late Jerry St. Jean, had a great reputation for youth football throughout New England. It was a source of pride to the many natives of my town who were connected to the church that bore the name St. Mary's!

329 St. Mary's

330 Over the course of the year, when my Dad came home from working at a grocery store, he and I went for a visit to the convent to bring food to the sisters!

331 As noted throughout this book!

Conversely, some of those towns, including the one in which I grew up, as well as its neighbors, now have buildings in which church services are held for congregations that never existed when I was growing up there. Yet, even with the explosion of some of these evangelical and independent churches, life in those towns really is not the same as it was back in the day, those days when Sunday morning church was a significant part of life for those who identified as Christians. *The times, they HAVE a changed and there is not a lot of turning back!*

YOU MAY SAY I'M A DREAMER [332]

To be clear, I do not think I am naïve enough to believe that things are going to turn around and we will have a major renewal in how religion is practiced in this nation. If we are looking for a return to the good old days, I don't expect those days to come back again.

Yet, there IS a significant difference between a desire for the good old days and the recognition that the church of the present day NEED NOT GIVE UP and JUST FADE AWAY.

If anything, this movement [333] called Christianity needs people who will answer the question posed by the title of this book and the words of this chapter: IS ANYBODY THERE? DOES ANYBODY CARE?

Is ANYBODY THERE who wants to discover that church can really make a great difference in the lives of young people, adults of all ages and the wider community?

DOES ANYBODY REALLY CARE about the value and purpose of this institution to which we give the name CHURCH?

You see… I am not prepared to support the loss of the Christian church. Not at all. To be honest, the possibility of that loss troubles me quite deeply!

If it were at all possible, I'd love to see people of all ages who have an interest in those things that truly matter in this life of ours,

332 From the song *Imagine,* John Lennon.
333 And I LOVE calling it " a movement."

find the value of gathering together for prayer and worship that both means something in their lives but which also has the capacity to make a difference in the lives of others.

So often, when people complain about the way things have been as in this case when so many people look back at this thing called church and declare how it turned them off, they really DO have a good point*:*

BECAUSE...

The church they have known is NOT the church it could be.
An awareness of that is good and it can lead us to ask even greater questions, all that lead ultimately to the questions that have driven the purpose of this book!
SO...

* *Do you see more possibility in the word church right now than you ever have before? Or is that word simply a remnant to you, a remnant from the past? I hope not BUT I respect your honest response!*
* *Can people answer those questions with the simple assurance that their answer and their willingness to live out the implications found in that answer will make a difference in their experience of faith and through the living out of that experience will make a difference in the lives of so many others as well?*

With that in mind, we finish then with the most important questions of all, questions about this institution that has existed for a couple of thousand years, this institution that has both nurtured so many people and frustrated so many others as well:
When it comes to the very existence of this community called church and its potential relevance in both this, our modern world, and in the future that lies ahead-
As we prepare to live in the present with our eyes gazing into the future, what do you think?

When the word CHURCH is spoken and people go back and forth about what it is and what it used to be, what goes through your mind?

When all is said and done and push makes way to shove, what is the church in your life?

Is it something of the past, teetering near the edge of irrelevance and demise or might it become something more as we face the years ahead?

In my view, as we move into the church's future, these are important, challenging and thought-provoking questions.

When we think about this word CHURCH and what it might mean in the shaping of both our personal lives and the life of our culture, what do we think? With all of its decline and its tensions, its shaky, complex history and its place in this, our modern world, the way I look at it, these are important questions for us to consider.

SO, IN CONCLUSION

For those of you reading this who find the church irrelevant or, even worse, an example of what religion should not be, I get it! I have felt that way myself sometimes! Yet, I hope that in these words that I have written and which you have read, there may be something that may cause you to consider ways in which this institution that goes by the name of church, founded on the life of an amazing man and possessing ideals all too often neglected, can move beyond its many flaws and live out those ideals through the inspiration and the example of the many human beings who, for one reason or another, have found great purpose within it over the course of time, who have found far more in the church than laws, cliches doctrines, dogmas and unhealthy religion, perhaps inspiring us to discover for ourselves a quite different vision of church, a vision inspired by the man whose name is Jesus!

SO HERE GOES THEN...

When it comes to this topic of church…
What do you think?

When it comes to this topic of church in our contemporary lives.........

IS ANYBODY THERE? DOES ANYBODY CARE?

I sure hope so...I hope that the institution we call church continues to remain relevant and does not simply fade into being seen as a remnant from a now long ago past. I hope that people driving or walking by those church buildings in their neighborhoods find something there that speaks to their experience of this mystery that goes by the name of LIFE!

I say this because for all its many, many flaws and despite my many criticisms that have grown out of my years of some interesting church related experiences, I nonetheless believe that the institutional church, if properly reformed, and most importantly, if FOCUSED on Jesus, has the incredible capacity and potential to make significant differences in the lives of those of us connected with it in any way.

In fact, it can make positive changes in both our nation and in our world, as well as changes in the ways in which we might perceive that which we call religion. These are changes, I would suggest, that we all too desperately need!

Please give this some thought and please find ways to engage in conversations with one another about the questions I have sought to raise in writing this book.

Thanks for reading this!

www.ingramcontent.com/pod-product-compliance
Lightning Source LLC
Chambersburg PA
CBHW021228090426
42740CB00006B/429